Index of Girls' Names

For Index of Boys' Names see inside rear cover

DEREK & JULIA PARKER'S

COMPLEAT ZODIAC NAME BOOK

The Guide to Your Name and Naming Your Child

William Luscombe

CONTENTS

First published in Great Britain in 1976 by William Luscombe Publisher Ltd
The Mitchell Beazley Group
Artists House 14–15 Manette Street London W1V 5LB

© 1976 by Derek and Julia Parker

ISBN 0 86002 079 7

Phototypeset by Tradespools Ltd Frome Somerset
Printed photolitho in Great Britain
by Ebenezer Baylis and Son Limited
The Trinity Press, Worcester, and London

INTRODUCTION

As far as we know, there has never been a man or woman without a name. The sounds by which men learned to tell one another apart were among the very earliest inventions in language.

If we could eavesdrop on our remote ancestors at the dawn of civilisation, we would probably find the names they called their children not only very odd, but very similar – we might scarcely be able to tell one 'name' from another, the difference between 'Ug' and 'Og'. But as language developed, and man slowly acquired the techniques of thought and speech, the giving of personal names to children (as opposed to 'family' names or 'surnames') became a very complicated matter indeed.

Perhaps the easiest way in which we can guess at those first efforts in name-giving is to look at the habits of the primitive tribes of our own century; and we find parents in them naming their children often for magical reasons – choosing names which they hope their children will grow to deserve: *Hope*, or *Constance*, for instance (in, of course, the language of the tribe or nation), But sometimes a baby will be given an ugly name, on purpose: he might be called *Filth* or she might be called *Ignorance*, so that the devils should think that they were not worth bothering with, and leave them alone!

Then, a tribe or family might name a child in commemoration of a famous event which they did not want forgotten (as if an English family might have christened a baby *Dunkirk*, in the 1940s, or an American family might call a boy *Moon-landing*!). In Old English, for instance, the name *Wystan* (used this century as the christian name of the poet W. H. Auden) means 'battle-stone', and originally commemorated a boy king of Mercia, murdered near a monumental stone.

The name might be in memory of a purely private incident or emotion: the Jewish name *Ben-oni*, for instance, is recorded in the Bible as being given to a baby born after a difficult labour in which its mother died: it means 'son of my sorrow'. In the *Morte d'Arthur* it is said that the baby *Tristan* was so-called because of the death of his mother, and the sorrow of his father in the event. (In fact, the name does not come from the French *triste* at all; this was a bad guess by the author of the book!)

Of course some names have simply been made up by parents who thought they sounded good – and this is especially true in America in the present century. Such girls' names as *Kathetta, Marilla, Elizene* are examples. Sometimes an elder brother or sister will contribute: the son of a friend of the authors invented the name *Ronanni* for his baby sister, and the parents christened her so. Other inventions sometimes come from novelists or poets: Shakespeare invented several names for his characters, including the bewitching *Miranda*; Sir Philip Sidney invented *Pamela* in 1590, for a character in his *Arcadia*.

Most civilisations developed their own habits in name-calling, often quite different from each other. 'Forenames' (only in Christian countries did they become known as 'christian names') in ancient Greece were strictly a family matter: the eldest son of a family was given the name of his father's father, and later children the forenames of other relatives. Later on in life, they were often given nicknames by their friends (or sometimes, enemies). The philosopher *Plato*, for instance, was really called *Aristocles* (after his paternal grandfather), but earned his nickname because – as one can see from the familiar little statue of him – he was *plato*, or 'plump'.

In imperial Rome, there was an extremely complex set of laws governing name-giving – in fact the system became so complicated in the end that a man might find himself with eighteen or twenty forenames! Slaves, of course, had no such problems, for they had no names – they simply took their owners'.

When Christianity was established in the West, a whole new group of names became extremely popular – the names of the Church's saints and angels. In the sixteenth century the influential Council of Trent insisted that all Christians should name their children 'christianly', and Biblical names became extremely common. But still the old names clung on (in personal matters, people resist change), and in a small village in the christian Europe of the eleventh century, one would come across a *George* living next-door to a *Pharamus*, with *Mark* and his wife *Hodierna* just across the way.

As far as the English-speaking world is concerned, the Norman invasion of England in 1066 was an enormously important event in the history of forenames; the Normans brought their own clutch of names with them, and these soon flooded out all the old English names with *Richards* and *Roberts* and *Ralphs*, *Williams* and *Walters* . . . *William, John* and *Thomas, Elizabeth, Mary* and *Anne* were the popular names of the twelfth and thirteenth centuries (over half the population of England bore them!); after the Reformation a fashion for Biblical names complicated the situation – or maybe simplified it, for there might often be fifteen Johns in one small village. Now the names of the characters in the religious plays performed on scaffoldings in the little town squares and on the village greens of the country, were given to new-born children; and the Crusaders brought back some from abroad, too.

The Puritans were particularly eager to mark their children off from the godless, and gave them seemingly outlandish names – *Rediviva* and *Desideratus* and *Beata*, together with even stranger ones such as *Praise-God* Barebones received at his christening.

In some parts of America, the effect of the strong Puritan influence can still be seen in the names of the inhabitants. In New England, for instance, *Joseph, Samuel, Joel* and *Ezra* are much more common than anywhere in England. Both in England and America, the habit of giving children two or three or more names grew in the early twentieth century, though there is still a difference in writing them: William L. Barnaby in America would more likely be W. Leonard Barnaby in England, or W. L. Barnaby; and he would be less likely, too, to be W. Leonard Barnaby, Jr.

In some countries in Europe, the law still keeps a paternal eye on christenings. In France, the Revolutionary Law of 11 Germinal XI, made in 1803, still decrees that names shall only be chosen from among those already recorded in history (Ronanni would have had no chance there); in Germany, a child may only be named by a name which can be proved to have been used before.

In England and America there are no such restrictions, though clergymen have been known to put their feet down about some of the more outlandish names chosen by recent parents. Among the hippy communities there has been a new plethora of delightfully strange and evocative names – which may perhaps lead to some embarrassment when the children are grown. The new interest in astrology has led to some children being named *Child-of-the-Stars* or *Moon-child* or *Planet-boy*.

But where does astrology come in, in the naming of children? The extent of its influence in all areas of life – from politics to art, from agriculture to poetry – has been so all-embracing that it would be strange indeed if it had had no effect upon that very personal matter, the naming of a new-born child.

It is sometimes very easy to see an astrological influence in the naming of a child, mainly through an association between the time of birth and the qualities of some well-known person born at that time. This is particularly so with religious forenames: in the thirteenth century, a girl born on 15th August would be named *Mary*, because that was the feast-day of the Virgin Mary.

But the little girl born on 15th August, 1203 – the first recorded *Mary* in England to be christened because of her date of birth – would not have had the characteristics of Virgo (the sign so obviously associated with the Virgin). She would have had at least some of the characteristics of the sign Leo (c24th July to 23rd August): magnanimity, perhaps; creativity and enthusiasm, optimism, and a flair for bringing joy into the lives of others.

Similarly, a boy born on or near 18th October might well be christened *Luke*: he would have some of the characteristics of Libra (c24th September to 23rd October): charm and a love of harmony, diplomacy, idealism . . . But there is of course no evidence that St Luke was a Libran!

The difficulty was of course that the Feast Day of a saint often had no connection with that saint's astrological characteristics; and there has never been an attempt to associate names with their astrological characteristics. That is the gap this book attempts to fill. Until now, the layman with no knowledge of astrological technique, who may have wished to give his child a 'suitable' name, could only make a guess – like the Greeks, who named their children for personal qualities they hoped they would develop, or the Celts who named their sons for the bravery and nobility they hoped they would grow to.

As the children grew up, nicknames often remedied the situation; and the astrological significance of nicknames is often very strong. How many Cancerians may have been nicknamed *Snappy* because of the shortness of their tempers? How many Capricorns *Meanie* because of their traditional care in money matters? But even then, the situation is complicated by the complex nature of astrology itself: the Sun-sign (which everyone knows, because it depends on the time of year one was born) is only one feature of the Birth

Chart, and not necessarily the most important. So a *Meanie* whose Capricorn instincts might come from his Rising-sign, might have a Leo Sun-sign, or *Snappy* might have his Sun in Virgo!

Sometimes, christian names are derived from ancient gods who have their astrological associations: *Martin*, for instance, comes from *Martius*, 'of Mars', and Mars was associated with the Greek God of War, Aries; and there are other gods too – various names beginning in 'Os', stem from a German god (*Oscar* = 'god' and 'spear').

This leads us to the way we have constructed this book. The first thing to say about it is that it is, of course, a book which is primarily for the layman. Astrologers often play games among themselves in which they may associate, say, a particular piece of music with an astrological sign (not necessarily one which is important in the Birth Chart of the composer). They would not pretend that they were making a very serious critical point. Nor would we say that it is important that a child born when the Sun was in Aries should be given an 'Arian' name.

But the mingled joy and perplexity of trying to think of a name for a baby to be born in a month or two is sometimes made keener by, say, the suggestions of friends, or one's memories of other *Toms*, *Dicks* or *Harrys* one has known. In this book we place as many christian names as we can think of, under the twelve astrological signs; parents who expect their child to be born when the Sun is in Cancer, might look at the list of Cancerian names, and there find something they like.

Those with a more specialist interest in astrology can play the game a little more finely! In natal astrology, the complete Birth Chart shows the position of all the planets in all the signs, plus the Rising-sign (that coming up over the eastern horizon at the moment of birth). They may like to wait until after the birth, and draw up the baby's Chart: they then have a much wider choice, for they can choose from the Sun-sign list, the Rising-sign list . . . or if the child was born when one of the planets was directly on the eastern horizon, this too could offer a choice: *Diana*, for instance, would be a splendid choice for a girl with a prominent Moon placed near the Ascendant! *Martin* would be an excellent name for a boy born when Mars was rising (the derivation is 'Man of Mars'!).

If you would like to commemorate a relative in naming your child, but perhaps do not enormously care for the relative's name, why not look under the sign which represents the grandfather or grandmother's Sun position, and take a name from the list there?

Since this is the first attempt made to list forenames astrologically, we have had to make our own rules. Fortunately, in most cases it was simply a question of going to the original meaning or derivation of the name: the grouping was then obvious. *Rachel*, for instance, comes from the Hebrew word for a *ewe* – so where could one place it but under Aries, whose symbol is the ram? *Justin*, in the original Latin, meant 'just' – a natural name for a Libran, preoccupied always with the idea of fair-play and justice.

In other cases, other means have been used: a name which seems to have no original meaning, but which was first widely used in a particular country, will have been placed in the sign which 'rules' the country concerned. Occasionally, when no other solution has offered itself, we have placed a name under the sign associated with the most famous bearer of that name – Winston is a case in point, which was placed under *Sagittarius* in commemoration of the birth of that famous Sagittarian Sir Winston Churchill.

In almost every case we have tried to make the reason for the grouping quite plain, though readers with an interest in astrology will perhaps be quicker to see this than the casual reader! You will find that browsing through the book you will pick up quite a keen appreciation of the characteristics and qualities of the signs, simply by the name-associations!

Finally, a plea: mothers- and fathers-to-be, *please* make a careful and accurate note of the *birth-time* of your children! (the sound of the first cry is the moment to take). In the U.S.A., Scotland, and some other countries, the birth-time is noted on birth certificates – but even these can sometimes be inaccurate, and a difference of as little as four minutes can make a radical difference when an astrologer is calculating the full Birth Chart, or map of the sky for the precise moment and time of birth.

Astrology is becoming more and more popular, and more and more respected. After a period of comparative neglect, doctors and psychiatrists in increasing numbers are realising that a professional astrologer can often offer considerable help to parents in forecasting the possible times of childish illnesses, or in suggesting the type of school a child will do best at. Astrologers often offer help in advising possible careers for school-leavers, and later in life with adolescent problems. If an accurate birth-time is not available, the work that can be done is extremely limited. And remember, if you do not want to consult an astrologer about John or Mary, John or Mary may later want to do so!

Derek and Julia Parker.

ARIES

21st March–19th April

ARIES

GIRLS

APPOLINE This unusual but pretty name was common in the fifteenth and sixteenth centuries, but has been used more recently, and in the U.S. (particularly New England) survived as *Abbelina* as recently as 1827. St Apollonia, a third-century Christian martyr, is invoked to cure tooth-ache.

APRIL The name of the month, used as a christian name in the twentieth century.

AVERIL From *Everild*, a seventh-century Yorkshire saint; but probably derived from the Old English, 'eofor hild' – 'battle with a boar'! This suggests a brave Arian.

BERENICE The Macedonians adopted the Greek term meaning 'bringer of Victory', which could scarcely be other than Arian! After the Reformation, it began to be used in England, mainly because of its appearance in the Bible.

BRUNHILDE The brave, independent heroine of Wagner's *Ring* (she was a Valkyrie in the ancient German legend from which he took the story) is most Arian of them all; the name originated from the old German *brunnia* (breastplate) and *Hild* (battle).

CAMILLA Camilla, Queen of the Volsci, was killed in battle by one of Aeneas' soldiers in Virgil's poem: an Arian warrior! The name became popular in England for a while after Fanny Burney's novel *Camilla* was published in 1796.

CLOTILDA The Old German Chlotichilda (from *hloda hildi*, or 'loud battle', was the wife of Clovis, King of France, in the fifth century; Clotilde is still common in France, and Clotilda is still sometimes used by English Catholic families.

DRUSILLA Drusus was the name of a Roman who slew the Gaul Drauses: an Arian, surely? Herod Agrippa named his daughter Drusilla, after one of the mistresses of Caligula. The latter would certainly have to be an Arian to stand up to him!

EILEEN Probably the Irish equivalent (Eibhlin) of Helen (see below).

ELAINE Also from Helen, this time in the Old French: often found in the old legends, and in Malory's *Morte d'Arthur*. After Tennyson wrote *The Idylls of the King*, and told afresh the story of Lancelot and Elaine, it became popular in England and America.

ELEANOR Sometimes, in America, Elinor; yet another derivation of Helen (see below). Eleanor of Aquitaine, the wife of Henry II, brought it to England, and Eleanor Crosses he put up in her memory recall her. Sometimes pronounced (in Victorian times) El-e-a-nor. Very popular in eighteenth and nineteenth century England, and often found in novels of the time (Jane Austen made Elinor Dashwood the heroine of *Sense and Sensibility*, and Little Nell in Dickens' *The Old Curiosity Shop* is really an Elinor.

ELLA Ella and Ellen are two final versions of Helen, both well known in England over the centuries, and Ellen especially popular in Ireland.

ESTRILD An unusual name, from the Old English Eastorhild, combining the name of the goddess of the rising sun, Eastre, with the word for *battle*. The sun is exalted in Aries.

EUNICE From the Greek, meaning 'fine victory'; but it appears in Acts and Timothy as the name of the mother of Timothy, and so became popular in Victorian times, with other Biblical names.

FREDA See Winifred (page 11).

GENEVIEVE Popular in France, especially because St Geneviève is the patron saint of Paris. When the Franks were blockading Paris, she led a convoy to run the blockade and bring food to the starving people: an active Arian saint.

GEORGIANA Derives from George (see page 13). Queen Anne persuaded the parents of one of her godchildren to christen the baby Georgiana – the first recorded use of the name. *Georgia* is the form most often used in America.

GINERVA The Italian version of *Guenevere* (see page 64). Used in England during this century.

GODIVA Her long hair saved the modesty of the well-known wife of Leofric of Mercia, who streaked engagingly through Coventry on horseback; her daring and her hair suggest an Arian. The name has unfortunately become too much of a joke to be used widely today, which is a pity.

GOODETH 'God's war', in the Old English; used regularly until the seventeenth century.

GRAINNE Sometimes Grania; but one thinks mainly of the famous Irishwoman Grainne O'Malley, who led opposition to the forces of Elizabeth I, and was an Amazonian Arian Princess.

HELEN The name became so popular in the West because of St Helena, traditionally the best-known English saint, and mother of Constantine the Great: Aries rules England. She may not have truly been the daughter of Old King Cole, but her name has certainly always been well-used since the Norman conquest, sometimes as Ellen.

HILDA From the Old English *hild*, meaning 'war' or 'battle'. Used since at least the seventh century, in England.

JESSICA A name invented by Shakespeare for the heroine of *The Merchant of Venice*, whose bravery in defying her father suggests Aries.

JOCELYN The name seems to be derived from an Old German name for the Goths, which would place it under Aries (which rules Germany).

JUDITH 'A Jewess' in Hebrew; the race is ruled by Aries. A King of Wessex married a Judith in the ninth century, and the name has been used since. Sometimes its pet-version, Judy, becomes an independent name.

KAREN The Danish form of Katherine (a Libran name); for many centuries purely Danish, however; therefore grouped under the sign that rules Denmark – Aries. Came to England from America, where immigrants took it.

LENA See Helen, from which it is derived.

LEONORA The origin is not clear: we place it under Aries in homage to the most famous Leonora, the heroine of Beethoven's opera *Fidelio*, who, dressed as a man, succeeded in rescuing her husband from a vile prison.

LINDA An ancient German name, not used in England until vety late in the nineteenth century. Germany is an Arian country.

LOIS Timothy's grandmother, in the Bible; but according to some authorities, derived from the Old German, 'famous war', and thus Arian. Like other Biblical names, commonly used in the seventeenth century, and now fairly popular in the U.S.A. and England.

MARCIA A Roman family, Marcius, derived their name from the god of war, Mars; indisputably a Martian family!

MARTINA See Martin (page 14).

MATILDA From the Old German words for 'strength' and 'battle'. William the Conqueror's wife was a Matilda, and the name was popular for several centuries; fell into disuse; then became fairly popular again.

MAUD The French version of Matilda (see above).

MAYA In some cultures, the goddess of Spring.

NELL Nell or Nelly is a corruption of Helen (see page 10), though the most famous Nell (Gwynn) was an Eleanor (also an Arian name).

NICOLA The Italian form of Nicholas (see below), but now often used in England; Nicolette is sometimes used too.

ORIEL Though best known in England as the name of an Oxford college, this German name (from *aus*, 'fire', and *hildi*, 'strife') was a girl's name in the thirteenth century, and is very occasionally still found.

PERSEPHONE The beautiful Greek name of the goddess of spring. Aries marks the spring equinox.

POPPY From the flower, most commonly an Arian red.

PRIMROSE From the flower which blooms when the sun is in Aries. Particularly popular in seventeenth century Scotland.

PRISCILLA From the Latin for 'former', which implies 'first': Aries is the first zodiacal sign. One of the difficult names to assign! Popular with the puritans.

RACHEL The Hebrew name for an 'ewe', and thus of course Arian. Formerly a popular Jewish name, but now used by all sects.

SIDONY A Roman Catholic name used in past centuries for girls born at or near the Feast of the Winding Sheet of Christ, when the sun is in Aries. Very few people can remember this derivation now.

SIRI In the ancient Norman, 'conquering impulse': Arians will be familiar with the instinct!

TILLY From Mathilda (see page 11).

UNA Una is an ancient Irish name which became Winifred in England (see below); Juno is another version, which Sean O'Casey used in his play *Juno and the Paycock*.

VALDA In the Old German, 'battle heroine'.

WINIFRED The original Winifred, Gwenfrewi in the Welsh, was a martyred Princess. When a passing chieftain, repulsed by her, struck off her head, the ground opened to swallow him, and her head joined itself on again; both the head (ruled by Aries) and the fate of the attacker suggest she was an Arian!

BOYS

ADAM This ever-popular name was used in England before the Norman conquest, as the name of a monk; in the twelfth century it became more and more popular, and eventually was one of the commonest names, particularly in Scotland. It lost ground a little after the fourteenth century, but came back in Elizabethan times, and recently has once more become popular. Why is it an Arian name? – from its derivation, not from the Bible, but from the Hebrew word for 'red', an Arian colour.

ANSELM A name brought to England by St Anselm, a Lombard who became Archbishop of Canterbury! Though never really popular, it had a revival in the nineteenth century. It derives from the Old German, 'ansi' (a god) and 'helma', (a helmet): a warlike, Arian notion.

ARCHIBALD A genuinely Arian name, for it derives from the Old German *Ercanbald*, meaning 'genuine', 'simple', 'bold'. It came into England before the Norman conquest, and took many forms, some of them fairly outlandish (Archembald, Erchebald, Herchembaut!) St Eorkenweald may really have been an Archibald. It became very common in Scotland, where both Archie and Baldie were abbreviations. The Campbells and Douglases in particular adopted it as a name; it had a certain vogue in England in Victorian times, becoming well known mainly through the title of a popular song: 'Archibald – Certainly Not!'

BALDWIN 'Bold friend', from the Old German; the Flemish traders brought it to England in the twelfth century, and it became a popular name, though more often a surname than a forename.

BORIS A very popular Russian name, meaning, simply, 'fight'. Came to England in the twentieth century.

BRENDAN Irishmen probably revere the name because it was that of Brendan the Voyager, who wrote so delightfully of his voyage to the Land of Promise in the Atlantic (actually the Canary Islands), rather than because, in Old Irish, it means 'stinking hair'! The association with the head places it under Aries.

CADWALLADER A famous Welsh name, from *cad gwaladr*, or 'battle leader'.

CALEB From the Hebrew, 'bold', 'impetuous'. Now particularly used in Scotland and the U.S.A.

CONRAD The name of a tenth century Saint: but the name, in Old German, means 'bold counsel'. Fairly often used in England, first in 1436.

DENIS St Denis (or Dionysius), converted by St Paul, is reputed to have carried his severed head at his own funeral service. Such attachment to the head can only be Arian! Went out of favour for some centuries, but has had a revival since the turn of the present century, and is now fairly popular.

DUNCAN The vision of the Old Irish *Dun-chadh* or 'brown warrior' is of an upright Arian: there were two early Scottish King Duncans, one of them murdered by Macbeth. Always common in Scotland, but fairly rare in England. Became Donnchadh in Ireland.

EGBERT From the Old English for 'bright sword', and the name of the first King of all England. The Victorians revived it, probably because of their love of religious names (St Egbert was a Northumbrian).

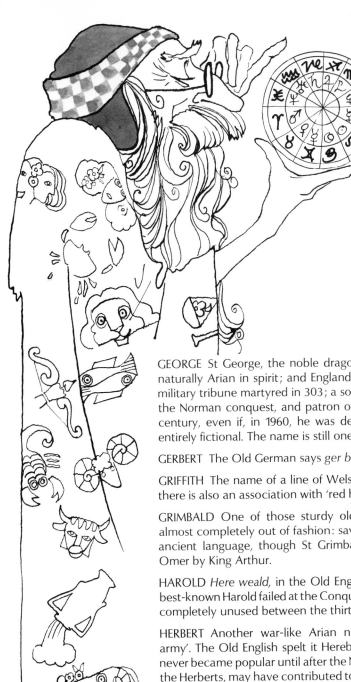

GEORGE St George, the noble dragon-killing patron saint of England seems naturally Arian in spirit; and England is ruled by Aries. George was a Roman military tribune martyred in 303; a soldier saint known in England long before the Norman conquest, and patron of England certainly since the fourteenth century, even if, in 1960, he was demoted by the Pope as being probably entirely fictional. The name is still one of the most popular in Great Britain.

GERBERT The Old German says *ger berhta*, or 'bright spear'.

GRIFFITH The name of a line of Welsh princes, and still often used in Wales; there is also an association with 'red hair', which suggests Aries.

GRIMBALD One of those sturdy old English names which has now fallen almost completely out of fashion: savage, fierce or bald is the meaning in the ancient language, though St Grimbald was a monk brought over from St Omer by King Arthur.

HAROLD *Here weald*, in the Old English, means 'powerful army', though the best-known Harold failed at the Conquest. The name, popular today, was almost completely unused between the thirteenth and nineteenth centuries.

HERBERT Another war-like Arian name, meaning in Old German 'bright army'. The Old English spelt it Herebeorht, which may be one reason why it never became popular until after the Norman conquest. A noble English family, the Herberts, may have contributed to its renewed popularity in the eighteenth century, though it never entirely went out of use.

IMBERT Not perhaps a very popular name these days, in fact little used since the fourteenth century; but ideal for an Arian, since it contains the Old German word for the Arian metal, iron.

JASON The Greek hero who pursued the golden fleece must have been sufficiently interested in the ram that bore it to be placed under his sign? The name is popular in the U.S.A., though now less so in England.

JERMYN From the Latin for 'a German'. Aries rules Germany.

JOCELYN See above, under girls. The name has always been used equally for both sexes.

JUDE In the Hebrew, 'Jehovah leads'. The concept of leadership is Arian. The connection with Judas Iscariot made the name unpopular for a while; Thomas Hardy's masterpiece *Jude the Obscure* did something to popularise it, but not for long.

KENELM The Old English meant 'brave helmet', suggesting a warlike Arian: a St Kenelm popularised the name in the English midlands, and some families there keep it alive today.

LEOPOLD 'A bold people', in Old German. Queen Victoria had relatives of the name, and it was occasionally used in England. The Belgian kings kept it alive in Belgium.

LLEWELLYN A common Welsh name, part of which derives from *llyw*, or 'leader'. The accurate spelling is Llewelyn.

MARCUS From the Roman family which took its name from the god of war, Mars. The name Mark derived from it, but is now so much associated with the evangelist that we have placed it separately, under Leo.

MARIUS Another derivation from a Roman family whose name was taken from Mars (it is Mario in Italy).

MARTIN The Roman family Martius, giving us Marcus and Marius, also gave Martin, which like the others is related to Mars, god of war. St Martin made it popular (he was a favourite saint in England), and it has always been used in English-speaking countries.

MAYNARD The Old German means strong and hardy, which suggests an Arian!

NICHOLAS 'Victory (for) the People!' suggests that the original Nicholas was an Arian; the saint, being the patron of pawnbrokers and wolves, is less instantly recognisable! The name was used in England well before the Conquest, and has been used ever since. Nick is a happy abbreviation. Colin perhaps originally came from Nicholas, but is now quite independent, and will be found under Gemini.

PASCOE Perhaps now more commonly a surname, Pascoe is associated with the paschal lamb, and with Easter (when the sun is in Aries).

REYNOLD Another of those christian names more common, now, as surnames: originally meant (in Old English) 'power' or 'might'.

RONALD The Scottish equivalent of Reynold (see above), and now far more common.

RORY 'The red' in the Gaelic. Red, the Arian colour.

ROY From the same root as Rory (see above) – *ruadh*. Originally Scottish, but now commonly used.

RUSSELL Originally from the French *roux*, 'red'. Probably more common nowadays as a surname.

SIDNEY Difficult to believe, but Sidney derives from Denis (see page 12)! – an etymologist will explain at great length. Sometimes used as a girl's name, and then sometimes spelt Sidony; but that has a separate derivation (see page 11).

SIMON The name was especially popular in the Middle Ages because of the cult of Simon Peter, the peculiarly Arian (impulsive, quick-speaking, touchy) apostle. The name also seems to have meant 'snub-nosed', which is associated with the head, ruled by Aries. Still a very popular name; sometimes reduced to 'Sim' (pronounced with a soft *i*) in past centuries.

THEOBALD 'Bold people', in the Old German, and just what most Arians are, in one way or another. A very ancient name; interestingly, Tybalt, in *Romeo and Juliet,* though he was probably a Scorpio, is derived from Theobald.

TRISTRAM From the Celtic 'tumult', and Arians certainly can be noisy folk. Sometimes written as Tristan (in Wagner's great opera, for instance), the name has been kept alive by the Arthurian legend, and has never quite died out, though it is perhaps less used today than it has ever been.

VICTOR 'Conqueror' in Latin, and being the name of an early pope and several martyrs, correspondingly popular. During the Victorian age it became popular in England, probably because people thought it had something in common with the great Queen's name. It has not.

VINCENT A popular third-century martyr roasted on a grill in Spain popularised the name there, and it came to England in the thirteenth century and has been popular ever since. 'Vince' is the extremely unpleasant diminutive. The name comes from the Latin *vincens,* 'conquering', therefore Aries.

WILLIAM This extremely long-lived and popular name (William the Conqueror brought it to England, where it has been used ever since) derives from the Old German words for 'will' and 'helmet', which suggests a forthright no-nonsense Arian. Goodness knows how Bill came to be used as the pet-name!

YOUR ARIES CHILD

Families with a young Aries in the house will certainly know about it. The lively, enthusiastic and sometimes rather boisterous qualities of Aries are forces to be reckoned with.

Aries children respond well to energetic and demanding projects and outings, and need to be given plenty to do to keep them busy – especially physically. A bored young Arian will tend to sit around and mope, being no good at all at pretending an interest in something which doesn't attract him or her.

Basically, they are straightforward and generally uncomplicated: what they say, they mean – and indeed they can be perhaps a little too outspoken at times. While they are young, this can be passed off as simple childish honesty, but the trait often hangs on well into adulthood, and perhaps a little correction and guidance will avoid embarrassments later.

The major Arian fault is selfishness. Should an Arian child be confronted with the prospect of a new brother or sister, parents must watch the behaviour pattern extremely carefully. The more he or she can be encouraged to help mother with the new baby, the better it will be, not only for Aries but for the family as a whole, for the Arian theme song does tend to be: 'Me first – me, me, me!' So a positive way must be found to develop this rather self-orientated motivation. 'Me first!' has negative and selfish tones, but they can be tuned to play a new tune, and to display the best Arian qualities – a pioneering spirit, and leadership, for instance.

There really does seem to be a pioneering element somewhere in all Arians, and it is interesting to see exactly in what area it comes to the fore. Arians are traditionally physically brave: but this can sometimes be manifested in bravery in developing their own life-style, in a choice of a career or hobby, or in developing one area of their lives in which a form of courage is needed – perhaps defending an opinion or outlook that may need determined advocacy.

Many young Arians are good at sport, and if there is talent for, say, the heavier ball-games, parents should give plenty of real encouragement and practical help. Arians have no objection to noise, so that even by today's standards records and radios and TVs will have their volume turned up to the full! Hobbies may involve the use of sharp tools, and it is more than likely that long-suffering parents will live a great deal of their lives to the background noise of clanging metal against metal, of power-drills and lathes and hammering. This mostly applies, of course, to the Arian boys – but the girls too can be 'fairy elephants', and even if they have a weekly dance class (a good excuse for them to burn up some of the abundant Arian energy, setting aside their cultural value) they can make a fair old din rushing downstairs, just by being themselves.

In their enjoyment of life, and of what they happen to be doing at any one time, Arians can become somewhat accident-prone, often suffering many minor cuts, bruises and burns; and as the head is the Arian area of the body, this tends to collect an above-average number of minor bumps. (Arians, by the way, either never get a headache, or suffer considerably from them. If they do, the cause can be a kidney disorder).

It is extremely important for parents of Arian children to help them develop patience. This may not be easy – but it should be born in mind, as they can sometimes be erratic, and sitting quietly still is to them one of the worst things in the world!

The Arian child has positive enthusiasm in plenty, but hobbies started with keen interest may fall by the wayside if they become too demanding or 'difficult'; Aries should be taught to *plod on* when this happens. In their quick, bright, able way, they can nevertheless be absent-minded. It is not always easy to counter this, but as they get older they usually learn consciously to pull themselves together, and the sheer tediousness of, say, having to spend hours on the doorstep because they have forgotten their keys is too much for any Arian.

Aries children enjoy spending their pocket-money, and their enthusiasm for something expensive will persuade them (with their natural enterprise) to take holiday jobs, do a paper round before school, or find some other way out of the problem. Any projects should be encouraged by parents; it is particularly positive for an energetic, keen Arian to achieve objectives by his own ingenuity.

School life for an Arian will probably be patchy. They make excellent progress in some subjects, and can be interested by practically any subject – but they can fight for the lowest position in class, and not care a bit about it, especially if they work with teachers they dislike or subjects they loathe. Parents who try to *make* little Martin or Judith learn their homework when they don't want to, will be banging their heads against a brick wall. But an Arian who loves a subject will be no trouble at all.

TAURUS

20th April–21st May

TAURUS

GIRLS

ADA Coming into England from Germany at the end of the eighteenth century, Ada became a popular name (Lord Byron christened his daughter Augusta Ada). It was last popular in Victorian England. Though sometimes a pet-name for Adelaide (an Aquarian name), it is really a Taurean derivation, for its source was the Hebrew *Adah*, 'an ornament' – and Taureans love decorations and possessions!

ALISON Sometimes a pet-name for Alice, it first became common in France, but was popular in England (particularly in the North country) by the eighteenth century. The Scots still love it. We take it to be Taurean because of its first notable appearance in English poetry, in Middle English:
From all women my love is lent
And lights on Alison!

AMARYLLIS First Greek, then Latin (you can find it in the poets Ovid and Virgil), and popular with English poets too – Milton, for instance. A name for a Taurean country girl.

ANTHEA The poet Herrick wrote several poems to Anthea, and so did many of his friends among the seventeenth century poets. They almost invented the name, though it comes originally from the Greek adjective meaning 'flowery' (hence, Taurus); it was never very common, though one writer in 1922 claimed to know 'two families in which for several generations it has been usual to call a daughter Anthea'.

APPLE The name of the fruit, sometimes used as a Christian name, could be nothing but Taurean!

BERYL The precious stone beryl belongs to a group ruled by Venus, the ruler of Taurus, which also dominates possessions of value. Its use as a christian name is fairly recent.

CAROL The association with music suggests Taurus. Most popular, still, in the southern states of America, though more recently also in England.

CECILIA The patron saint of music could exist under no other zodiacal sign! William the Conqueror named his daughter Cecilia, and popularised the name. Fanny Burney's novel *Cecilia* popularised it anew in the eighteenth century. It becomes Ciss, or Sis, for short.

COMFORT Occasionally used as a christian name, even as recently as the nineteenth century; popular especially with the Puritans. Taureans love comfort.

DOREEN Originally an Irish derivation from Dorothy (see below), which came into use in England after the publication in 1894 of Edna Lyall's novel of the same name. Now very popular indeed.

DOROTHY Dorothy or Dorothea, from the Greek 'gift of God', was a fourth century saint who, on her way to her execution, met a lawyer who mocked her, asking her to send him flowers and fruit from the heavenly garden. Whereupon a child miraculously appeared with a basket of apples and roses. The lawyer, Theophilus, promptly became a Christian. The association with flowers and fruit also associates Dorothy with Taurus. The name becomes Doll and

Dolly. In the seventeenth century Doll became a name for a loose woman, and at about the same time became the name for a child's plaything, a doll. Dot, Dodo, Dora are also used.

DAGMAR From the Danish, 'joy of the land'.

EARTHA Made famous by the singer Eartha Kitt, the name seems simply to mean 'of the earth': Taurus is the first earth sign.

EMERALD The name of a precious stone which, like the beryl, falls under Taurus.

EMILY Or Emilia; and the latter was the heroine of a tale by Boccaccio which Chaucer took up in his *Knight's Tale*: she was a very beautiful lady, 'and like an angel sang a heavenly song'; clearly, a Taurean!

FLEUR From the French noun, 'flower', and made famous by Galsworthy in his *Forsyte Saga*.

FLORA The Roman goddess of flowers; the name, adopted in France, was especially popular in Scotland, and still is: such heroines as Flora Macdonald helped to keep it well-used.

FLORENCE Oddly enough, originally a man's name; now used only for women, and originally from the Latin *florens*, 'blooming' – again, an association with the flowers loved by every Taurean. Sometimes becomes Florrie, Flossie or Flo.

GEMMA 'A gem', from the Italian; Taureans particularly love precious stones, Gemma Galgani is a modern saint, who only died in 1903, and perhaps renewed the name's popularity.

HANA The Japanese name for a flower.

LEAH Unflatteringly, the Hebrew for 'cow', and certainly Taurean! The Puritans used it a great deal, as did of course the Jews.

LINNET This charming name was popularised by Tennyson, who used it in *Idylls of the King*; the Victorians took it up. Placed here because of the association with the song-bird.

MAVIS An old popular name for the song-thrush used for the first time by the immensely-read novelist Marie Corelli, and now popular.

MAY Associated with the month during which the sun is for the most part in Taurus; derived, though, originally from Margaret or Mary (see Cancer and Virgo respectively).

MERAULD An old Cornish name, from emerald, a Taurean stone.

MERLE The Latin name for a blackbird; Merle Oberon the filmstar, made it fleetingly popular in the '30s.

MIA From the Italian meaning possession: 'mine'. A very Taurean feeling!

NELDA From the Scandinavian for 'elder', a Taurean tree.

PATRICIA The feminine version of Patrick (see page 21), first used in Scotland in the eighteenth century; one of Queen Victoria's daughters popularised it in England.

REBECCA Much used by Jewish families, and as a christian name after the seventeenth century; here because, in the Hebrew, it signifies 'a heifer'!

Thackeray's heroine, in *Vanity Fair,* was 'Becky', which is sometimes still used as an abbreviation.

RHODA 'A rose' in Greek; Taurus rules roses (though *white* roses fall under Cancer!).

ROSA From Rose (see below).

ROSALIE *Rosalia,* in Latin, was the annual hanging of wreaths of roses on tombs; roses are ruled by Taurus.

ROSE The flower-name has become so associated with this name, that it would be perverse not to place it under the sign which rules roses. But there is a theory that the name really came from *hros,* the horse: and that would suggest Sagittarius. So one can take one's choice. Still an enormously popular name, after a thousand years of use in England.

VERDA From the Latin, 'blooming', an impression given by many Taureans.

VIOLET A Taurean flower.

BOYS

BARTHOLOMEW St Bartholomew no doubt prompted the name Bartholomew in old England. But the name derives from the Hebrew 'abounding in furrows'! – so has a peculiarly Taurean earthy origin.

CHENEY From the Old French, 'from the forest of oak trees': solid, dependable, reliable, and thus Taurean.

CRISPIN From the Latin Crispinus, or 'curly': Taureans' curly hair is a special trademark for them. The brothers Crispinus and Crispinianus, martyred in 285, are the patron saints of shoe-makers, so perhaps Pisces has a claim here!

DONALD One of the most common Scottish names, used also in Ireland, and not unsurprisingly from the ancient Celtic: *dubno walos,* 'mighty (in the) world'. This seems to hint at a strong Taurean. Donal is often the Irish form.

DWAYNE Almost exclusively used, now, in America: from the old gaelic for 'poem' or 'song' – Taurus is the sign most associated with music.

ELLERY 'Of the elder trees', in Old German; they are ruled by Venus, which also rules Taurus; and the elder flowers in May.

FLORIAN 'Flowery', 'blooming', in the Latin; the name of a Roman saint, but Taurean because of the association with flowers.

FOSTER A corruption of 'forrester': a Taurean occupation.

GAWAIN Sometimes becomes Gavin: here because of the association with *Mei,* the month of May, rather than because of *gwalch,* the Welsh for 'hawk', and the first syllable of the name. Sir Gawain, of the old legend, seems to have been remarkably handsome, anyway! – and Taurus is traditionally the best-looking sign.

HERCULES With his great physical strength, Hercules (son of Zeus and Alcmena) must surely have been a Taurean. (His Labours, incidentally, can be matched to the twelve signs). An English christian name until the seventeenth century, and used in Cornwall until the nineteenth.

HUMBERT Originally meant 'giant', and most popular in Italy (Umberto), and in Germany – but sometimes in England and America. Nabokov's Humbert, in *Lolita,* is perhaps the most famous fictional example (a Scorpio?).

KEAN An Irish name, derived from the word for 'vast': making one think of some bullish Taureans. Ireland is also ruled by Taurus.

LUKE St Luke prompted the wide use of this name, and his symbol in art is the ox, suggesting Taurus. Now somewhat out of fashion, though often used during the last century in England and America.

NIGEL Unsuccessful attempts have been made to trace this name to its beginning; but all that is clear is that it is Irish, so it arrives here by virtue of Taurus ruling that country. It travelled from Ireland to Iceland, then to Scandinavia, then to France, then to England with the Conqueror, and has been popular ever since.

OSCAR Another name difficult to trace, but again indisputably Irish, so under Taurus for that reason. Never very widely used in England; the downfall of the most famous Oscar (Wilde) made it unpopular, and it has never really recovered.

PATRICK Patron saint of Taurus-ruled Ireland, and so mainly an Irish name, though popular too in Scotland, and lately in England. Finding a New York policeman not named Patrick was for some years difficult! – though there were also a few Mikes (see Gemini).

ROGER Somehow, during the Middle Ages, Roger was almost always the name of an agricultural labourer! – and Taureans love working on the land, or in their gardens. Roger fell out of use in Victorian times, because of a lewd association, but is now back in favour again.

YOUR TAURUS CHILD

The Taurean child is pleasant, kind and reliable – a type needing above all else to be allowed to develop very gradually at his or her own pace. It is essential that they are not rushed or confused by over-anxious parents who may think that progress at school is perhaps too slow. Indeed, when this is compared to that of brothers and sisters it may be the case – but the most important thing to remember with Taurean children is the fact that as long as progress is steady and they plod their way through school subjects, perhaps rising a few places each term, all is well. It will be wise of parents to accept the fact that, generally speaking, the Taurean boy or girl will not make sudden leaps from the bottom of the form to the top. If they do, then this should be looked upon as a pleasant surprise; it must not be *demanded* of them. 'Slow but sure' is the right way for Taureans. It is not impossible, however, to find a rather lazy streak in the Taurean child; he may prefer sitting around, or doing anything relaxing, to getting on with homework or important tasks. Parents really must be on the look out for this; such remarks as 'Oh, I'll do that *tomorrow!*' could become very common indeed, and should be discouraged at all costs.

It is important to remember that Taurus has the reputation of being 'a good-looking sign'. Taureans do have a natural charm – sometimes to the point that they can get away with anything! Taurus is very often musical, and Taurean children should always be encouraged to play an instrument and to sing. The school choir is often an excellent starting-point for this activity, and should little Rose or Crispin be given a solo on speech day, their talent should be nurtured with care and given a great deal of sensible but not too gushy encouragement.

All Taureans have a tendency to become over-weight, and this trait soon makes its presence felt in the children. At its best we have the Taurean babies who are no trouble to feed at all – they just love every mouthful from the first suck; but at its worst in childhood the Taurean will tuck away far more sweets and candies than most other types. This obviously is not good either for shape or teeth, and must be checked. Under stress, in particular, the Taurean child is most likely to raid the cake-tin.

The most negative Taurean trait is possessiveness, which should be corrected from an early age. It could become something of a problem if younger brothers and sisters come on to the scene, or, of course, when young Taurus realises that he has his own possessions. He may not want to share his toys very much, and may cling on to them, underlining the fact that they are *his*. The need for material success will soon show in an interesting way in the Taurean child – pocket money will be spent with great care, and financial decisions taken with considerable deliberation. Usually, the Taurean child is marvellous in this respect: putting aside a little money each week for holidays will not be difficult. But it is important to learn to use a little of that precious hoard to buy tiny presents for other members of the family.

The Taurean child will thrive – perhaps more than any other type – in a secure background. He needs a very regular pattern to his life; any domestic upset will irritate him, for he must know exactly where he stands, and what is going to happen. A real sense of security is essential, and disruption or a change in that pattern could be distressing. It is important to explain any family changes slowly and carefully; the Taurean child will then come to terms with them in his own way, and in a delightfully philosophical manner.

Taureans do not dislike routine and discipline, and generally speaking will accept them as very much part and parcel of life. They often lean towards the conventional, and this is probably why a school where the discipline is on the strict side is good for them, as they usually thrive in this atmosphere rather than that of a school with a more liberal attitude to education.

Young Taureans may have to be encouraged to take exercise to burn up their energy. Once involved in sport they can do extremely well: more creatively, music, as already mentioned, is excellent for both sexes; the girls are usually very good at slow crafts such as embroidery; both sexes should do well at sculpture and design. Mathematics should be encouraged: this could be extremely useful later on – many Taureans find themselves gradually heading for the top in banking and accountancy.

GEMINI

22nd May–20th June

GEMINI

GIRLS

ANASTASIA The youngest daughter of the last Tsar of Russia was the most notable Anastasia of our own time: some say she still lives. Born on 17th June, she was a Geminian, so we commemorate her here, though the original Anastasia was said to have been the Holy Virgin's midwife, and there might be an argument for placing her name under Cancer for that reason! A very popular name in England during the Middle Ages, and still popular in Ireland, as a translation of the Irish *Aine*.

BEATRICE or Beatrix: from the Latin, 'bringer of joy' – the happiest of messengers. Became Bettrys in Wales, and Beaten in Cornwall. In the 'literary' nineteenth century the name, which had almost died out, became popular again because of its literary associations – Shakespeare's Beatrice, Dante's Beatrice. Now sometimes nastily pronounced 'Beetriss' – really, of course, Bé-á-triss; never one hopes, Beat!

BERTHA From the Old English 'bright', and often used in England after the Conquest, right up to the nineteenth century.

CHLOE The Greek original means 'a young green shoot', suggesting Geminian freshness and liveliness. St Paul mentions a Chloe, and the fashion for Biblical names made it popular. A favourite in Southern America.

CRESSIDA The original seems to have meant 'faithless' or 'fickle', which certainly suggests Gemini! As a name, it first appears in Boccaccio (as Chryseis). Chaucer called a character Criseyde; Shakespeare turned her into Cressida when writing the story of her betrayal of Troilus, and made her a by-word for faithlessness.

DEBORAH Became a popular name in the seventeenth century, when the puritans used it a great deal. Originally from the Hebrew for 'a bee' – bees are busy as any Geminian! Milton named his youngest daughter Deborah. In Mrs Gaskell's *Cranford* Miss Jenkyns insisted on its old pronunciation, Debôrah.

ECHO Any talkative Geminian is likely to repeat herself!

ESTHER The Persian equivalent of the Hebrew name for myrtle! According to the herbalist Culpeper, the myrtle tree is ruled by Mercury, which also rules Gemini.

EULALIA From the Greek, 'silver-tongued'; Geminians are certainly generally that. Spain and France use the name more than the English-speaking nations, but Cornwall sometimes adopted it.

EVE Or Eva. From the Hebrew, 'lively', and naturally Geminian. In the Bible, the name of the first woman, Geminians would no doubt claim that her behaviour with the apple suggests Scorpio! *Uncle Tom's Cabin* led to a revival of the name in America.

EVELYN The Old English is 'dear youth', and Gemini is the most youthful of the signs, mentally and often physically. Evelina was used by Fanny Burney as the heroine of the novel of that name, and popularised as a girl's name what had previously been chiefly a boy's.

FAY A modern name, which probably came from the old word for a fairy or elf: Morgan le Fay, in the Arthurian legends, was really a wicked fairy. The quickness and lightness of the little people suggests Gemini.

FENELLA From the beautiful Gaelic word *Fionnghuala*, or 'white-shouldered'. Gemini rules the shoulders.

FLAVIA A Roman name, from *flavus*, yellow: a Gemini colour.

GILLIAN In the Middle Ages, when the name was most popular, it became Gillot or Jillet, and was often used to suggest a flighty, unfaithful girl: Geminians usually have some duality in their love-life.

GRACILIA From the Latin *gracilis*, 'slender' – Geminians usually have no weight problems, and keep their slim figures.

GWYNETH A favourite Welsh name: Gemini rules Wales.

HEBE From the Greek 'youth', so belonging to Gemini, most youthful of signs.

HERMIA From Hermes, who was the messenger of the gods, and as Mercury rules Gemini. Shakespeare may have invented this version for *A Midsummer Night's Dream*.

HILARY Geminians usually preserve a certain cheerfulness, and 'cheerful', in Latin, is *hilarius*. As Hilaire, popular in France; used in England during the thirteenth–sixteenth centuries, and since then for both sexes. Hilaire Belloc the best known recent example.

JAY From the Old English, 'lively', and perhaps also associated with the crow; both concepts suggest a lively and talkative Geminian. The name is more popular in the U.S.A. than England, though *The Great Gatsby* revived it for both countries at the same time. Sometimes used as a boy's name.

JILL Originally, a pet-name for Gillian, now often used independently. For the astrological association see Gillian, above.

JUNE Like other names from the names of months, this one has only been used since the turn of the century. The Sun is in Gemini for most of June.

LALAGE An uncommon (but still current) christian name, from the Greek for 'babble'. Can any Geminian deny the association?

LETTICE From the Greek *Laetitia* (still often used in that form), or 'gladness', which strongly suggests the typical Geminian gaiety. Lettice was popular in the nineteenth century, Laetitia in Victorian England.

MEHITABEL 'Activity' is associated with the Aramaic original of this name; and one is reminded too of the rather Geminian confidante of Archie the cockroach, in Don Marquis' irresistible saga.

MELISSA In the Greek, a Geminian bee – but also a nymph.

MIGNON From the French for 'dainty', which, at their best, Geminian girls are.

MYRTLE The myrtle tree is ruled by Mercury, the ruler of Gemini, according to the herbalist Culpeper.

PAULA The feminine form of Paul. (page 27).

PAULINA Another feminine version of Paul.

ROBINA The feminine form of Robin. (page 27).

SIBYL In ancient Greece, the sybils spoke as representatives of the gods; their utterances were prophetic. No one could fail to associate speaking with Geminians, who never seem to close their lips; a fairly common name in the Middle Ages.

TABITHA This delightful girl's name, very popular in England around the seventeenth and eighteenth centuries, is Aramaic, and means 'gazelle', the most graceful of Geminian quick-movers.

TAMSIN See Thomasin.

THOMASIN A diminutive of Thomas (see page 28); so is Thomasina, which is sometimes used. Tamsin is a name still to be found in the English west country.

TRILBY From the Scandinavian, 'giddy, frivolous', which is a Geminian idea; and Trilby in George du Maurier's famous novel seems a Geminian character, too. She made the name briefly popular in the nineteenth century.

TRIXIE From Beatrice (see page 24).

TRYPHENA 'Dainty' or 'delicate' in the Greek, which are Geminian characteristics. Used quite often in the sixteenth and seventeenth centuries; now uncommon, but occasionally found in the West country of England, and used by the novelist Thomas Hardy.

VICTORIA Though the name means 'victory', which suggests perhaps Aries or Sagittarius, the name is placed here because of the overwhelming influence of the great Queen, who in fact had not only her sun in Gemini, but Gemini rising as well, and showed many of the characteristics of the sign. Oddly enough, the name was never quite as popular as one might have expected, and now seems uncommon.

VIVIENNE The French and feminine form of Vivian (see page 28). Tennyson, in a poem, anglicised it as Vivien, but the former spelling seems pleasanter.

BOYS

ANGEL From the Greek for 'a messenger': Mercury was the messenger of the gods, and rules Gemini. Angel only became a personal name fairly recently – in the thirteenth century – and spread from Byzantia and Sicily to Italy, France, and finally to Cornwall, where it was used as a man's name from the sixteenth century onwards. Thomas Hardy used it in *Tess of the D'Urbervilles*; Angel Clare was Tess' husband.

ANEURIN The name of a Welsh, and doubtless Geminian, bard or poet, who lived in about A.D. 600, and gave his name to many Welshmen, including the Socialist politician who gave England her National Health Service. Anciently spelt Aneirin.

BALLARD Probably from the Latin, 'babbler'! Geminians never stop talking.

BERTRAM The Old German *berhta hraben*, or 'bright raven'. Both brightness and the talkativeness to which ravens can be prone suggests Gemini! Last popular in the 1920s in England; P. G. Wodehouse's Bertie Wooster may be the last of the breed?

CLARENCE In 1362 Edward III created the Dukedom of Clarence for his third son, who may have been a Geminian, for the name comes from the Old English for 'bright light'. The most famous Clarence was drowned in a butt of malmsey by his brother, Richard III. Popular until the middle of the last century.

COLIN The Scots version of the name comes from the Gaelic for 'a gay young dog!' The English version comes from France, and is really an abbreviation of Nicholas, an Arian name. In the sixteenth century it was thought to be low-class, and eventually died out; but then it spread down from Scotland, and became popular again.

EVELYN Still occasionally used as man's name: the derivation is from the Old English 'dear youth', and Geminians usually still look young at 85!

EWEN A Scottish christian name, from the Gaelic *Eoghan,* a youth (see under Evelyn).

GARETH Sir Gareth, in the Arthurian legend, finally threw over his many-coloured tunics, and settled for a yellow habit – which suggests a Geminian trait somewhere. As Gary, often used in the U.S.A.

GIDEON Originally one of the Judges over Israel: in the Hebrew, the name means 'having only a stump for a hand'. Geminians must beware of accidents to the hands and fingers, which suggests that the original Gideon must have been more Geminian than was good for him. Still a popular name in America.

HILARY See page 25.

IVOR Sometimes spelt Ifor, and a very Welsh name, so we place it under the governing sign of that country.

MALACHI While no one could claim that Malachi was a popular twentieth-century christian name, there could scarcely be a more Geminian one: it means, in Hebrew, 'my messenger'! In Ireland, Malachy is sometimes used; Maelaghlin was an Irish saint.

MATTHEW The symbol of the apostle was an angel, the 'heavenly messenger', associated with Gemini through Mercury, the messenger of the gods, who rules the sign. The Normans brought the name to England, and it has been popular ever since.

MICHAEL One of the archangels, or God's messengers (see under Matthew above for angels and Geminians). There are nearly 700 churches in England dedicated to Michael, showing how popular the name once was; indeed, still is. Mike, Mick and Mickey are the unspeakable ugly derivatives.

NEVILLE In the remote French past, from *nouveau ville,* or 'new town'; the busy-ness of town, and the newness, both strongly suggest Gemini.

OWEN Wales is governed by Gemini, and Owen is a common Welsh name (whose actual origin is obscure).

PAUL Popular because of the saint, who seems Geminian for several reasons – notably the fact that on the road from Tarsus he suffered the most radical change of mind even the mercurial Gemini could undergo; and the fact that he never stopped writing letters, most Geminian of occupations. An extremely popular name throughout the whole of Christendom over two thousand years.

RAPHAEL One of the archangels, Geminian in character (see under Matthew, above).

ROBIN Gemini rules birds, and it is this association which sticks, though the name more accurately derives from the Virgoan Robert.

THOMAS Thomas is placed under Gemini for two reasons: not only does it actually mean 'twin' in Aramaic (and Gemini is of course the most positively dual of the zodiac signs), but the best known of all Thomases was the Christian Doubting Thomas, and Geminians are notable sceptics! The name has been used in England since well before the Norman conquest, and has never fallen out of popularity.

URIAN A Welsh name meaning 'town-born'; Geminians commonly prefer dwelling in towns to living in the country.

VIVIAN From the Latin word meaning 'alive', which suggests Geminian liveliness and intensity of life.

YORICK 'I knew him well, Horatio . . . a fellow of infinite jest.' Yorick, the king's jester, in *Hamlet*, seems to have had his name invented by Shakespeare.

XAVIER In the Aramaic, 'bright'; brightness, both in spirit and in mind, is an attribute of the best kind of Geminian.

YOUR GEMINI CHILD

Another name for young Gemini could well be young Chatterbox! Parents of Gemini children really do need to be walking encyclopaedias, ready with a quick answer for everything. To satisfy young Gemini, each question must be clearly and concisely answered, and if there is a loop-hole out will come another question to supplement the first. However, Gemini isn't really interested in the depth of a subject or a problem – that may be their failing – having an insatiable appetite for *knowing*, and for talking – non-stop. This trait doesn't usually end with childhood, either. It is important for Geminians to be allowed to express their very natural duality quite fully. 'One thing at a time, dear', is *not* good advice for Gemini children; they do not function at their best that way. They really need to have several hobbies on the go at the same time, need to be reading more than one book, and so on. This can pose problems for the parents of Gillian or Colin, because they are notoriously restless, and conversely can become easily bored.

The best way to treat a Gemini child is to let them have a lot of things to do, and to let them change as frequently as they feel they want to, from one occupation to another. Firmness must be shown in making quite sure that each project or task taken on is really completed, otherwise a lot of effort can be wasted, and Gemini will leave a trail of unfinished models, half-written stories or thank-you letters, and so on, in his or her wake. It is essential that Gemini is not allowed to become bored, and indeed it is often out of boredom that restlessness develops. A teacher who is slow or not very interesting will not impress Geminians at school; a subject that doesn't stir the imagination or, more importantly, a subject that is put over badly by the teacher, will be one in which Gemini will have poor grades at the end of term. Gemini at school needs discipline, but needs freedom – the freedom to question why things have to be done in a specific way at a specific time. Being by no means unreasonable, Gemini will accept the discipline if it is logical; it is to this natural logic and to a lively mind that parents should appeal.

Parents may well find that the Gemini child will work in fits and starts rather than plodding along at a steady pace. This will be reflected in school reports, and the infuriating phrase 'Could do better if he/she tried!' has been known to occur all too frequently – though there is really no lack of enthusiasm.

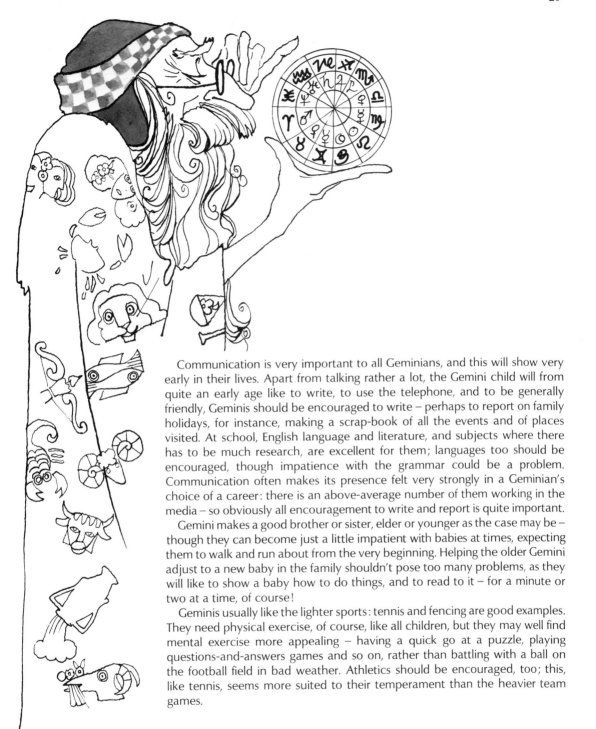

Communication is very important to all Geminians, and this will show very early in their lives. Apart from talking rather a lot, the Gemini child will from quite an early age like to write, to use the telephone, and to be generally friendly, Geminis should be encouraged to write – perhaps to report on family holidays, for instance, making a scrap-book of all the events and of places visited. At school, English language and literature, and subjects where there has to be much research, are excellent for them; languages too should be encouraged, though impatience with the grammar could be a problem. Communication often makes its presence felt very strongly in a Geminian's choice of a career: there is an above-average number of them working in the media – so obviously all encouragement to write and report is quite important.

Gemini makes a good brother or sister, elder or younger as the case may be – though they can become just a little impatient with babies at times, expecting them to walk and run about from the very beginning. Helping the older Gemini adjust to a new baby in the family shouldn't pose too many problems, as they will like to show a baby how to do things, and to read to it – for a minute or two at a time, of course!

Geminis usually like the lighter sports: tennis and fencing are good examples. They need physical exercise, of course, like all children, but they may well find mental exercise more appealing – having a quick go at a puzzle, playing questions-and-answers games and so on, rather than battling with a ball on the football field in bad weather. Athletics should be encouraged, too; this, like tennis, seems more suited to their temperament than the heavier team games.

CANCER

21st June–22nd July

CANCER

GIRLS

ADRIENNE A female version of *Adrian* (see under *Pisces*): but the general meaning, 'woman of the sea', strongly suggests the mother which is so strong a Cancerian element in astrology.

ALEXANDRA The female form of *Alexander*, a strongly Cancerian name, became popular in England when the Prince of Wales married Princess Alexandra of Denmark during Victoria's reign – though the name is found seven hundred years earlier! Interestingly, *Alexander* was used as a girl's name as late as the seventeenth century.

ALMA The Latin adjective meaning loving, or kind, suggests Cancer; though oddly the name became popular in England for very unCancerian, warlike reasons: because of the battle of Alma, and the river Alma, in the Crimea.

ARABELLA A Scottish name (Scotland being a Cancerian nation): the first notable Arabella was the daughter of a Lord of Leuchars in the twelfth century. Arabella's friends sometimes called her Arbell; and though the name is unknown in the rest of Europe, *Orable*, as a man's name, is found in French history. Then, Arabia was sometimes known as Arrable! But it is not very likely that there is any connection with the Scottish name, which is not now (alas) very popular.

BRENDA A name from the Shetland Islands, which are governed by Cancer. It may have come from Norway, and *Brand*. In 1821, Sir Walter Scott called one of the heroines of his novel *The Pirate* Brenda, and caused great interest in the name, which rapidly spread throughout England and to America.

BRONWEN From the Welsh, 'white breast' – Cancer rules the breasts. Most common still in Wales, or with Welsh families.

CLARISSA Originally from Clara, a Sagittarian name. But we look to Cancer in this case because this version is so romantic: Clarice was a name which ran right through the old French romances – she was the wife of Rinaldo and the sister of Huon of Bordeaux. And Richardson, thinking of this, revived the name as Clarissa in his novel *Clarissa Harlowe*.

CLARIMOND Claremond and Esclairimonde appear in ancient romances, and Clarimond was a Devonshire name in the seventeenth century. It originated from a mixture of the Old German *munt* and the Latin *clarus*: the idea of 'protection' is one which is always to the fore with Cancerians, who love to protect their family and loved ones.

CORAL The origin of coral in the sea suggests an association with Cancer.

CYNTHIA One of the names of the goddess Artemis, who protects against all evil: nothing could be more Cancerian. In the seventeenth and eighteenth century it became very popular in England and America, especially after Mrs Gaskell's novel *Wives and Daughters*. America really adopted it; England came to it rather later.

DAISY Started out (as most people now forget) as a pet-name for Margaret (marguerites are daisies). So see page 33.

DELIA The connection is with Artemis (because of her birthplace, Delos); so see Cynthia, above. A favourite name particularly with eighteenth century pastoral poets: but still found today.

DIANA Most people think of Diana the Huntress, which certainly might suggest Sagittarius; but the name is really that of the moon goddess (Artemis, in Greek), and the moon is of course ruled by Cancer. Never a very common name, but a favourite with novelists (Scott, Meredith used it for famous heroines in *Rob Roy* and *Diana of the Crossways*).

DORIS In Greek mythology, the name of a sea nymph, which is certainly Cancerian; but seems to have been used as a christian name only for about 200 years.

DULCIE Probably from the Latin *dulcis*, 'sweet.' Only found during the past century or so, though Dowsabel was very popular in France in medieval times.

ETHEL In the nineteenth century this name suddenly appeared from nowhere, and there have been many discussions about its origin. Most etymologists now agree that it probably comes from Ethelberg, which in Old English meant 'a noble fortress', and suggests the Cancerian's protective abilities. Many Victorian novelists used the name, which has been popular ever since.

EUSTACIA The feminine version of Eustace (see page 35).

FIONA Fiona Macleod was a character invented by the novelist William Sharp in the late nineteenth century, and the name also seems to have been his invention. He took it from the Gaelic *fionn*, meaning 'fair' or 'white,' so it clearly has a Cancerian ring.

GERDA An ancient Norse name, but in modern times best known as the name of the heroine of the Hans Anderson story *The Snow Queen*, who is the very best kind of Cancerian child!

GRACE From the Old German adjective, 'grey,' a Cancerian colour. A Roman Catholic name during the seventeenth century; sometimes, then, a boy's name too. The heroine Grace Darling renewed its popularity in the nineteenth century.

GRETA An abbreviation of 'Margaret' (see page 33).

GRISELDA The Cancerian colour, grey, places this name (in its Old German origin). Chaucer used it in *Canterbury Tales,* and it has been around ever since.

HARRIET Derived from Henry (see page 35); the French invented the name, and brought it to England when Charles I married Queen Henriette Marie. Very common since then: sometimes called Hatty.

HENRIETTA Another derivative of Henry (see page 35; and under Harriet).

HERMIONE Though the name derives from Hermes (see under Gemini), it only became well known in England after Shakespeare had used it in *A Winter's Tale*: and that Hermione seems certainly Cancerian.

HORATIA A derivative of Horace (see page 35); Nelson and Lady Hamilton named their daughter Horatia.

IMOGEN May be from the Old Irish for 'daughter', or just 'girl', which suggests Cancer. Popular in the twentieth century, taken from Shakespeare's *Cymbeline*, and the result of a printer's error: he really wrote Innogen!

JOSEPHINE See Joseph (below) from which it is derived. Popular after the rise to power of the Empress Josephine (who in fact was not christened Josephine at all, but Josephe!).

JULIANA St Juliana was popular in the Low Countries (her relics were preserved at Brussels), and came to England in the twelfth century. Cancer rules the Low Countries.

LESLEY The feminine spelling of Leslie (see page 36).

MADGE Derived from Margaret (see Margaret below).

MADRA From the Latin: 'mother'. Cancer is the most motherly of the signs.

MAGGIE See Margaret, below.

MAISIE A Scottish nickname for Margaret (see below).

MALVINA Invented by the Scottish poet James MacPherson, perhaps from the Gaelic words meaning 'smooth brow': the latter is a special sign, often, of a Cancerian influence.

MARGARET In the Greek, 'a pearl', and Cancer rules pearls. The name was popularised by St Margaret, the virgin martyr who (or so an eye-witness claimed) was swallowed alive by a dragon. There were four other St Margarets, one of them being the eleventh century Queen of Scotland, so the name was much used there as well as in England. Margot, Madge, Meg, Maggie, Maisie are occasionally used; and the German Greta and the Italian Rita, sometimes.

MARINA From the Latin *marinus*, 'of the sea'. The woman monk, St Marina (once accused of being a father!) was known in the East, and the name was occasionally found in England in early times; but it was the beautiful Princess Marina, Duchess of Kent, who brought the name alive in England in this century.

MARTHA The patron saint of housewives could be under no better sign than that of home-loving Cancer.

MINNA Cancerians usually have very good memories, and as the Old German *minna* meant 'memory' the name seems to fit here. Used in Scotland; Sir Walter Scott wrote a novel (*Minna Troil*) which took it into England.

MONDAY In the Middle Ages, a child born on a Monday was sometimes given the name; Monday is of course Moonday, and the moon rules Cancer.

MORWENNA This beautiful name comes from the remote parish of Morwen-stow on the north coast of Cornwall, where St Morwenna is the patron saint. Nothing is known about her; but her name perhaps comes from the Welsh *morwaneg*, 'a wave of the sea', and Cancer is the sign most associated with the sea. A lovely name worth reviving.

MURIEL Sometimes (and perhaps preferably) spelt Meriel, the name means, in Gaelic, 'the bright sea', and seems to have occurred first in Brittany. It seems to have come to England with the Normans, and was never quite obsolete.

MYRA Derived remotely from the Latin for 'pearl', which places it here.

NEOMA From the Greek, 'light of the new moon'; Cancer is much associated with the moon.

NERISSA From the Greek: 'of the sea'. Cancer rules the sea. Shakespeare used the name in *The Merchant of Venice*.

OLWEN In Welsh (and it is a Welsh name) means 'white track'; there is an ancient legend of an Olwen so pure that when she walked, white flowers sprang up behind her. (She had, no doubt, a Virgoan influence in her horoscope!).

PEARL Cancer rules pearls.

PHILADELPHIA We suppose no American would dare christen his daughter Philadelphia; but it was a popular name in England as late as the nineteenth century, and means 'brotherly love', which suggests Cancer. (It is from the Greek).

RENÉE The feminine of René, from the Latin *renatus*, 'born again'. *Not* derived from Irene.

ROSAMUND 'Horse' and 'protection' in the Old German! On the whole, the protection idea seems dominant, which suggests Cancer (rather than the horse, which suggests Sagittarius. But take your pick.)

SANDRA The Italians invented this name as a short-cut for Alessandra; so see Alexandra (page 31).

SALENA From the Greek word for 'salty', suggesting the sea, and therefore Cancer.

TARA From the Celtic, 'a tower', and occasionally used as a girl's name (though most famous probably as the name of Scarlett O'Hara's home in *Gone with the Wind*.) The idea of a protective, guarding tower is Cancerian.

WANDA Originally, a German girl's name, meaning 'stock' or 'stem', and suggesting a preoccupation with family trees and genealogy which is peculiarly Cancerian.

ZELDA Derived from Grizelda (see page 32).

BOYS

ALEXANDER From the Greek, 'defending men' – and one of the Cancerian's traits is to look after and defend family and friends. Alexander the Great made the name enormously popular, naturally; in the British Isles, the Scots took it particularly to their hearts (it became 'Sandy', of course); the three King Alexanders of Scotland helped to make it one of the commonest of all Scottish names (in Inverness in 1894, there were 363 Alexanders!) Alec and Alex are other diminutives of this noble name.

ALEXIS Again from the Greek 'helper', 'defender' – Cancerian traits: and St Alexis was the son of a rich Roman who became a beggar, sharing all his goods with his friends. Especially common in Russia, and had something of a vogue in the rest of Europe when the great Russian novelists Tolstoy and Dostoievsky were first read there.

ANDREW Versions of Andrew are found in Latin, French, Italian, Spanish, German, Dutch, Russian and Greek! The patron saint of Scotland, he must surely have been a Cancerian? Jesus' first disciple probably had the Hebrew version of the name; he certainly made the name popular, and in England alone in the Middle Ages, 637 churches were dedicated to him. As a name for an ordinary man, Andrew became popular as late as the twelfth century; Scotland used it, in particular, shortening it sometimes to Andy.

BRUCE Scotland is ruled by Cancer, so the name of its most celebrated hero, Robert the Bruce, belongs here. The great liberator lived in the late thirteenth century; during the Middle Ages the name spread all over the British Isles, often becoming a surname.

CAESAR While the nobility of the great Julius Caesar suggests, perhaps, Leo, there are many Cancerian hints: Pliny, the historian, said the name originated because Caesar was born by a caesarian operation; another authority suggests the name originates from the Latin *caesius*, meaning 'bluish-grey' – both being Cancerian colours. If it truly comes from *caesaries*, 'a head of hair', then one would have to turn to Aries. But we stick with Cancer! It was a common name in Renaissance Italy, and a couple of saints of that name spread it further. The famous Sir Julius Caesar, Queen Elizabeth I's doctor, brought it to England, when it was used sparingly. There was a Julius Caesar Thompson in London, as late as 1799.

CAVAN From the Irish, 'comely birth'; birth and motherhood are especially Cancerian.

CHESTER From the Latin, meaning 'a fortified camp', and thus the name of an English city: the protective Cancerian idea again.

DWIGHT The John Dwight who emigrated to New England in 1635 gave his surname, through his many daughters, as a christian name to a large number of boys. Cancer is a sign which prompts love of family and many children, so the name seems to belong here. President Eisenhower was the latest, most famous bearer of the name, and it is hardly ever found in Europe.

EDWARD Edward the Confessor, one of the greatest English kings, and the last of the line of King Arthur, gave this name an impetus which has lasted until now. His care for his people was certainly Cancerian, even if the name did not come from the Old English *ead ward*, or 'happy guardian'. One of the very few English names to have become popular in non-English-speaking countries. Nicknames: Ned and Ted.

ESMOND A combination, in the Old English, of 'beauty' and 'protection', both of which fit Cancer very well. Thackeray's *The History of Henry Esmond* revived this very early name for our time.

EUSTACE From the Greek, 'fruitful'; if any sign tends to prompt large families, it is Cancer! The name was moderately popular in the first quarter of this century in England, but has died out since. St Eustace is the patron saint of hunting, so Sagittarius may have a claim.

GARTH Somewhat popular in the U.S.A., perhaps because of a strip cartoon. The name comes from the Scandinavian word for an 'enclosure', and Cancerians tend to 'collect' or 'encircle'.

GRAHAM The name of a well-known and large Scottish family, and Cancer rules Scotland. Only used as a christian name comparatively recently.

HAMO From the Old German for 'house' or 'home'; of all signs, Cancerians are most interested in home-building. Tends now to be a gypsy name.

HARRIS 'Son of *Henry*' (see below).

HARRY Diminutive of Henry (see below).

HENRY In the Old German, 'ruler of the house or home', and while the first part of the phrase suggests perhaps a Leo, the emphasis on the home is certainly Cancerian. All the ruling King Henrys in England kept the name popular. Harry used to be regarded as the correct name, and Henry as rather formal or old-fashioned.

HORACE Horatius, who defended the Tiber bridge in song and story, is the root of this name; and defence is a Cancerian activity. The poet Horace made the name popular, though the Victorians became confused as to whether this, or the derivative Horatio (Lord Nelson's christian name) was the most noble. Horace, on the whole, won.

JOSEPH In the Hebrew, an indication of a large family; Cancerians are generally much concerned with the home and family. Popular (like most Biblical names) in England since the Middle Ages.

KEITH A Scottish name, originally a place-name; so, under Cancer, for Cancer rules Scotland.

KENNETH From Scotland, the name having been used there since the first King Kenneth died in 860.

KENWARD In the Old English, 'a brave guard', suggesting the protective qualities of the best type of Cancerian.

LESLIE Originally predominantly a Scottish, therefore a Cancerian, name; though recently used in all parts of the English-speaking world.

MORGAN Very popular, always, in Wales, the name in part derives from the Welsh *mor*, the sea; and Cancer, more than any other sign, is associated with the sea.

MURDOCH In the Gaelic, *Muireadhach*, or 'man of the sea'. Cancerians will usually find themselves attracted to the wide ocean.

OMAR In Arabian, 'the ship-maker'; the name, of course, of Khayyam, whose *Rubaiyat* was made famous in Edward Fitzgerald's translation; a few admiring Englishmen christened their sons Omar. But not, it must be admitted, many. The sea influence places the name under Cancer.

OSMOND 'A protecting god', in Old English; now more often a surname (notably, of a famous family of light entertainers). The notion of protection is particularly Cancerian.

RANDAL *Rand*, in Old English, is 'shield', giving the Cancerian idea of protection. The name is particularly associated with the gipsy Smiths, Bosses, and Lees.

RAYMOND From the Old German, *mund* meaning 'protection'; *ragan* is 'wise' or 'mighty', so there is the idea of the quintessential protective Cancerian at his most determined.

RENÉ An attractive French name now sometimes used in England, and meaning 'born again'; the idea of newness, of rebirth is especially Cancerian.

RUFUS Though red is the Arian colour, it is often true that Cancerians have red hair; so we place this name, from the Latin for 'red-haired' here.

SCOTT Quite simply, 'a Scot'; and Scotland is a Cancerian country. Scott Fitzgerald is perhaps the best-known Scott of his generation, though the name is quite often used still in the U.S.A.

SELWYN Perhaps from the Old English for 'a friendly house'? If so, Cancerian;

for Cancerians love their homes, and love welcoming friends there. Fairly common in Wales, still, and occasionally elsewhere.

SWITHAN St Swithan was a bishop at Winchester in the ninth century, and it is legendary that whatever the weather is on his feast-day (July 15) it will remain that way for the next forty days. July 15 falls plump into the period when the sun is in Cancer (though in England the rain that often dampens his day might suggest Pisces).

TEDDY Diminutive of Edward (see page 35), and also sometimes of Theodore.

WALLACE One of the best-loved of all Scottish names (and Scotland is Cancerian); originally a surname, but used as a christian name after the hero William Wallace, in the thirteenth century.

WARREN From the Old German, and thought by some etymologists to have meant 'a dweller near an enclosure'; the enclosure suggests the protectiveness which is a Cancerian characteristic.

ZEPHANIAH In Hebrew, 'God has concealed'. Well, Cancerian wives will certainly be used to 'concealing' things from their husbands – we mean, by hoarding them, for Cancerians are great collectors. A husband named Zephaniah will not be likely to dissuade them; and anyway, the name is now uncommon!

YOUR CANCER CHILD

The Cancerian child could well be described as 'Little Mother' or 'Little Father'. One of the best qualities of the Cancerian, which really begins to make its presence felt from a very early age, is protectiveness, and parents of a young Cancerian will very soon notice that this delightful instinct will be expressed towards other members of the family – and not only younger members. Indeed, it is by no means impossible for the little Cancerian boy to express a very serious desire to 'look after Mummy' – especially if Daddy has to go away for a while. This delightful trait should be allowed plenty of expression, for it is necessary to the psychological development of the Cancerian not to be thwarted in this very basic instinct. If there are no other children in the family, the feelings could well be expressed towards the family cat or dog.

Parents have to be a little careful that the Cancerian child does not become too much of a stay-at-home, for in expressing the natural protective instinct they also develop an above-average need to be protected, and the psychological security gained from being at home and within the confines of a house and garden is considerable. It is self-defence, and Cancerians really do have a tremendously powerful self-defensive system which bristles every time they are challenged.

Changes of mood are also a powerful element of the Cancerian personality, and it is very easy indeed for the Cancerian child to give way to tears to get what is wanted; once this ploy works, it will be exploited to the fullest – so parents may run into some difficulties there! The Cancerian baby may not take too easily to being weaned, and indeed the Cancerian child will probably go off food, or develop digestive difficulties or slight sickness, if at all worried. It is a good plan, then, for the parents, should they find little Coral or Alexander unwell, to find out if there are school worries or problems, before visiting the doctor. It is also the case that the Cancerian child will look rather pale. This is quite natural, as they can have very sensitive skins. An above-average amount of protection against the sun when on holiday is strongly recommended – the wearing of a sun-hat and a light shirt in addition to applying lotions could well be necessary.

The Cancerian instinct 'to collect' will also develop in very early years. The boys' pockets will be even more full of treasures than most boys', and both sexes will hate to go through their toy-cupboards to throw out and tidy. This results in the illogical hoarding of all sorts of rubbish, and is not an easy problem for parents living in small homes! However, it can be guided into a marvellous interest, for we thoroughly recommend that all Cancerians from the earliest years should be encouraged to form a real collection of . . . well, it could be almost anything that takes their fancy! Sea-shells would be ideal; and postage-stamps; miniature dolls perhaps, for the girls (though some care is needed here, for the mother-instinct is so strong that if they are too much encouraged to play the feminine role it could cause some psychological conflict, and even feelings of guilt later, when it comes to career decisions). Anything old will attract, and 'things from Grandmother' will be looked after and carefully treasured.

History could well be a favourite subject at school, providing channels for exploration by the extremely active Cancerian imagination. Indeed, all subjects requiring the use of imagination are excellent for Cancerian children. They can do extremely well at school, for once interested in a subject their natural tenacity comes into play and they stick at it. At school, too, they can show their sensitivity by being easily hurt; conversely, to protect themselves they have, like the creatures of their sign, extremely tough shells – if they learn to harden them, they will do extremely well and become truly delightful people (especi-ally to those who learn to get through to their charming 'real' inner person-alities). Cancerian children will enjoy visits to all sorts of museums and art galleries, and it is important for parents to make additional efforts in that direction; they will be well rewarded. The boys will specially love industrial archaeology, and old steam engines and motor cars could well form part of a schedule to stimulate the Cancerian imagination.

LEO

23rd July–22nd August

LEO

GIRLS

ABIGAIL Leo, the sign of the father, and also of joy and pleasure, is associated for this reason with Abigail, which in Hebrew means 'father rejoices'. A very well-known name in England in the sixteenth and seventeenth centuries, it fell out of favour when Beaumont and Fletcher made an Abigail a chief character in their play *The Scornful Lady*, and as a result the name became associated with servants. At the same time, Abigail Masham, a favourite of Queen Anne, became extremely unpopular, which reduced the name's appeal. In America, especially among the early Puritan settlers, it remained popular, especially in its pretty diminutive, Abby.

ADELE The popular version (originally French) of the Old German name Adela, meaning 'noble', and thus especially Leonine.

AUGUSTA Associated nowadays with Oscar Wilde's impeccably Leonine Aunt Augusta in *The Importance of Being Earnest*, the name is out of fashion. In Victorian England it was popular, sometimes shortened to Gus or Gussie: it derives from the adjective *august*, 'majestic, venerable'. Also Leonine adjectives!

AURELIA From the Roman *aurum*, 'gold' – a Leo metal. One etymologist in 1655 translated Aurelia as 'little pretty golden lady', and Leos can generally be relied upon to have some gold about them.

AURORA The Latin goddess of the dawn, or the coming of the Leo Sun. The English, Germans and French used it, but not recently.

CHARLOTTE The feminine form of Charles, associated with the idea of king-ship, and therefore Leonine. It seems to have been coined for the wife of Louis XI of France, and came to England in 1626 with Charlotte de la Trémouille, who married the Earl of Derby. George III's Queen made it popular in the eighteenth century. It was once pronounced 'Charlotty', and Lottie is a pet-name from it.

DAPHNE The name of the unfortunate nymph loved by Apollo and turned into a bay-tree: Leo rules the bay (and laurel wreaths often crown Leonine heroes). In Victorian times most often used as a name for pets, but this century often used as a christian name.

DARICE From the Persian: 'queenly'. Nothing more Leonine!

DAWN Only used in this century, generally in popular women's novels; but attractive none-the-less, and the rising of the Leo sun plants it firmly here!

DOMINICA Given to children born on a Sunday (see Dominic, page 44): Leo is the sign ruled by the Sun, and therefore associated with Sunday.

EDEN 'Delight', in Hebrew. Another popular Biblical name.

EDITH In the Old English, *ead* (rich or happy) and *gyo* (war). Though Aries obviously has a claim, perhaps the name is more predominantly Leonine, with the implications of a conquering hero. St Eadgyth, a daughter of King Edgar, made the name popular in England as long ago as the tenth century. It never went entirely out of fashion, though it only became really popular again in the nineteenth century.

ELSA The heroine of Wagner's *Lohengrin* drew her name from the German for 'noble maiden'; a blonde lioness!

ERICA The feminine version of Eric (see page 44).

EUGENIA From the Greek 'excellence': nothing but the best for Leos. The Empress Eugénie made the name popular in France, and it is still sometimes used in England.

FREDERICA The feminine version of Frederic (see below).

GENE See *Eugene*, page 44.

GERALDINE As the feminine equivalent of Gerald (see below), this name was invented by a poet, the Earl of Surrey, in 1540, as a name for a beauty he was celebrating in verse.

GLORIA In Latin, 'glory', a Leonine attribute. Used as a christian name only in the past century.

HERA The Greek 'queen of the gods'; no queen could avoid Leonine traits!

HORTENSIA From the name of a great Roman family; and for want of other hints, placed here under the ruling sign of Rome. Hortense is sometimes used.

HOSANNA One of the names used by Puritans after the Reformation in England. While its original meaning was 'Save!', it has been regarded for centuries as a shout of praise: Leos love praise – and, to do them justice, praising. Very occasionally, a man's name; more usually, a woman's.

JULIA The feminine form of Julius, predominantly a Roman name, thus under Leo (which rules Italy). Though it was used by various poets (notably Herrick) before the eighteenth century, it is only since then that it has been a common christian name. In America, Julie (the French version) is common.

JULIET Shakespeare made it famous: adapting it from Giulietta, a diminutive of the Italian Giulia, or Julia. See Julia, above.

KINBOROUGH From the Old English for 'royal fortress', which describes perfectly the Leonine regal self-satisfaction at its least engaging!

LARA From the Latin, originally: 'famous'. Popular after the publication of Pasternak's *Dr Zhivago*, and the film made of it.

LAURA An obscure name, but some authorities believe it to have been derived from *laurus*, a bay tree; a Leo tree. Petrarch's mistress, incidentally, was Lora. Laura was popular in Wales for a long time; more recently, in England.

LEONIE A lioness, for the name is directly derived from Leo (see page 45); in fact Lioness was once used as a christian name! Leonie is French in origin.

LORNA R. D. Blackmore invented this name for the heroine of *Lorna Doone*: she was not only brave, steadfast, noble, but actually also of an aristocratic family; so it is difficult to believe she was not a Leo!

LOUISE Sometimes Louisa; and the French feminine version of Louis (see page 45). Quite popular in the eighteenth century; still fairly so today.

MARIGOLD A Leo flower.

MAXINE Very popular in France, this name has spread somewhat to England and America; it is the feminine of Max, so see under Maximilian (see page 45).

MIRABEL *Mirabilis*, in Latin, means 'wonderful' or 'glorious', so there is no hesitation in placing the name under Leo! In Congreve's *The Way of the World* it is used as a man's name, but this is exceptional.

MONA St Mona was an Irish saint, and the name was popular there; it travelled to England in this century. Its derivation is from the Irish 'noble'.

NEDA A Slavonic name for 'Sunday's child', Sunday being of course governed by the sun, which rules Leo.

NORMA The name has been used in England for at least seven hundred years, becoming especially popular through performances of Bellini's opera *Norma* (one of Queen Victoria's favourites). The name means 'rule', making it a good Leo placing.

ODETTE From Ottilia (also a Leo name, see below); but one remembers Princess Odette, from *Swan Lake*, certainly a Leonine bird!

OLIVE Sometimes as Olivia (see *Twelfth Night*) the name is derived from the Leo-ruled olive; two St Olives helped to keep the name popular through the ages.

OTTILIA Now an obscure name, meaning originally 'fatherland'. Ottoline is occasionally used: a famous patroness of the arts, Lady Ottoline Morrell, was famous in Edwardian England, and was the most leonine lady the authors have ever heard of!

QUEENIE A pet-name derived from Queen; Leo, of course!

REGAN Derived from regal, or kingly; thus, Leonine. *King Lear* provides us with the worst kind of Leo holder of the name.

ROMA The Italian capital's name is sometimes given as a christian name; a Leo-ruled city.

ROMOLA Derived from Romulus, the founder of Rome.

ROSEMARY The plant is ruled by the Sun, which also rules Leo; a very recent name – the first example dates from only 1745.

ROXANE From the Persian for 'dawn'. *Roxana, or the Fortunate Mistress*, in Defoe's novel, is a good example of an extrovert Leo.

RUBY The Leo precious stone.

SABRINA 'A princess', though also thought to be derived from the river Severn, in the English West Country. The first meaning would certainly place the name under Leo.

SALLY Derived from Sarah (see below).

SARAH In the Hebrew, 'princess', and an example of Leonine royalty. A common English name since the Reformation.

SHARON From *Sarah* (see above).

STEPHANIE From *Stephen* (see page 46).

TAMARA A Russian Jewish name, originally meaning 'palm tree'; Leo rules palm trees.

TIFFANY Though the name is derived from Theophania, the New York associations seem to place the name firmly under Leo; just as, if a girl happened to be christened Harrods, she would be associated with the same sign!

VERENA A martyr specially venerated in Switzerland; we therefore associated her with Leo, which rules that country.

YEDA Hebrew: 'heart's ease'. Leo rules the heart.

ZENOBIA The famous Palmyra Queen who bore the name sounds sufficiently Leonine; the name was used in the English West Country.

BOYS

ABNER Always popular in America, Abner comes from the Hebrew 'the divine father is light', and the 'father' image is a Leo one, even if the most famous early Abner had not been the commander of his cousin Saul's army!

ABRAHAM *Abram*, meaning in Hebrew 'high father', suggests Leo. Never very popular in England, it became Abram and Bram in the Low Countries, and after the Mayflower reached America became popular there – no doubt remaining so because it was Lincoln's christian name; its diminutive form, Abe, is particularly ugly, but nearly always used.

ALARIC Leos love to rule, and *alaric* in Old German meaning 'ruler of all', there is no difficulty in attributing this name. Popular as a name for Kings in ancient times: Alaric I demolished Rome in A.D. 410.

ALBERT The noble and misunderstood Prince Albert had many Leonine characteristics, which did not altogether marry well with Queen Victoria's Geminian ones; but the name is really associated with the Old German *athal berhta*, 'noble and bright', which sounds Leonine enough. Albert was a German, and the name was common there before it reached England (like the Christmas tree) with the Prince, and became especially popular among the poor. While in England, Alberts become 'Bert', in America they are usually 'Al'.

ALROY More popular in America than England, *Alroy* derives from the French *roi*, the King, and all Leos have their kingdoms.

BASIL From the Greek: 'kingly'. Basil the Great, a bishop and doctor of the fourth century, relentlessly put the rich in their place and befriended the poor. Popular in England in the 1920s, but no longer so.

CAROL Much the same origin as Charles (see below). Very common in the U.S.A., and recently in England.

CHARLES The true derivative seems to be from the Old German *carl*, 'a man' – but man at his noblest, and soon associated with the whole idea of leadership and kingship: a Leonine conception indeed. Charlemagne, or Charles the Great, dignified and popularised the name in Europe. Naturally it was very popular among Royalists during the English Civil Wars; but only became really common in the nineteenth century, often as Charlie.

CUTHBERT The Old English meaning is 'famous and bright', and the idea of a brave, bright hero is obviously Leonine! St Cuthbert, the English shepherd who settled in Ireland, popularised the name in the British Isles, though in the 1914–18 war, sadly, it became a nickname for a cowardly evader of military service.

CYRUS From the Persian word for 'throne', suggesting Leo kingship. Most often used in America.

DEREK The Dutch form of Diederich in German, or Theodoric in Old German (see page 46). Popular in England during the last half-century, sometimes spelt Derrick.

DOMINIC Sometimes Dominick, from the Latin 'of the Lord', and originally given to boys born on the Leonine day, Sunday. Used often for monks in Anglo-Saxon days, then used in honour of St Dominic, who lived in un-Leonine poverty, and founded the Order of Preachers.

DUDLEY Originally a surname for the powerful, Leonine Dudley family, which rose to great power in Tudor England. Became a christian name in the nineteenth century.

EAMON See *Edmond* (see below).

EDMOND Or sometimes Edmund; and from *ead*, 'rich', and *mund*, 'protection', in the Old English. Though Cancer obviously has a claim through the protective element, the idea seems to be of a powerful rather dominant lord, more Leonine in style. Edmund the Magnificent, King of England in the tenth century, gave the name to a series of English families. Now, in Ireland, Eamon is regularly used.

ELROY Mostly used in the U.S.A., and originally from the Latin, 'royal'.

EMERY From the Old German for 'ruler'. Used both for men and women for centuries, but now rare.

ERIC There is a connection with the Teutonic 'ruler' or 'governor', which gives the Leo rulership too. The Danes brought the name to England, but it died out until the nineteenth century, when Dean Farrar's successful school story *Eric, or Little by Little* repopularised it for our time.

EUGENE From the Latin term for 'noble' or 'well-born', thus indisputably Leonine. Four Popes took the name. Now, especially as Gene, it is popular in the U.S.A.

FAIRFAX Originally a surname, but occasionally used as a christian name, and deriving from the Old English for 'yellow-haired' – like, in fact, the lion.

FREDERICK From the Old German *Frithuric*, or 'peaceful ruler', which every Leo aspires to be. The nickname Fred came very early: there was a Fred de Tilney as early as 1360! Freddy is sometimes used, too. Always popular in England and the U.S.A.

GENE See Eugene, above.

GERALD If Leos cannot rule peacefully as Fredericks, then they will rule forcefully as Geralds (from the Old German *Gairovald*, or 'rule with a spear'. Went out of use in England fairly early, but was kept alive in Ireland, and reintroduced to England in the nineteenth century.

HOWARD As a christian name, used only very recently; the surname may come from the Old German *hugu vardu*, or 'heart' and 'protection'. Protection may be Cancerian, but the idea of committing oneself heart and soul (another meaning of *hugu*) is Leonine.

HUGO From the Old German, 'heart'; Leos are all heart. The name came to England with the Normans, and has been popular ever since (St Hugo of Lincoln helped: a child martyr).

ISAAC The sense, in Hebrew, is that the bearer will welcome one in a friendly manner; and Leos have an approachable friendliness, however noble they may be (or think themselves).

ISAIAH In the Hebrew, 'Jehovah is *generous*' – a very Leonine trait. Used as a christian name for at least three centuries.

JETHRO The Hebrew for 'abundance' or 'excellence', and as such, undoubtedly Leonine! Popular for a while in England, but now mainly so in America.

JONATHAN 'God has given a son', in Hebrew; Leo is the traditional sign of the father and of the son – in other words, the masculine element. A name particularly attractive to the Victorians, with their theories of ideal male friendships (referring to the story of David and Jonathan's love for each other).

JOSHUA 'Jehovah is generous.' Leos have a great sense of generosity – though they also expect it. From the same root as Jesus, which, though a popular christian name in Spain and South America, has very rarely been used in English-speaking countries.

JULIAN From Julius (see below): there have been ten St Julians, so it is not surprising the name was popular until comparatively recently. Galsworthy converted the name (it was sometimes spelt Julyan) to Jolyon for *The Forsyte Saga*.

JULIUS The name of a Roman family of great fame: Leo rules Italy. Julius Caesar made the name popular for some time after his death, but also in Victorian England.

KENRICK 'Royal ruler', the Old English says; little used since the 17th century.

LAURENCE Sometimes spelt Lawrence, the name originally meant 'a bay tree' in the Latin; bays are Leo trees. There were various monkish Laurences in England before the conquest (after St Lawrence of Canterbury), and it has been a mildly popular name ever since.

LEO Thirteen popes bore this ultimately Leonine name. It has become in the U.S.A. a favourite Jewish name; in England, is more used by Catholic families.

LEONARD 'Bold lion', in Old German, and firmly Leonine! St Leonard was a favourite saint, and helped popularise the name.

LEWIS Sometimes spelt, in the French manner, Louis. The origins of the name are somewhat Arian ('to hear' and 'to fight' in Latin); but it is too much associated now with King Louis XIV, 'the Sun King', to be placed anywhere except under the care of Leo, which the sun rules.

LIONEL The French made this name as a version of Leo, 'the lion' (see above).

MAGNUS In the Latin, the name means 'great'. Magnus I was a King of Norway, and seems to have had his name invented by servants as a version of his real name, Charlemagne (*Carolus Magnus*). Several Scandinavian kings bore the name, which later became popular in Scotland and Ireland.

MARK Marcus is the name from which Mark originally came, and it will be found under Aries. But the artistic symbol of St Mark is the lion, which hints that a Leo placing would not be much out of the way.

MAXIMILIAN More often simply 'Max', the name falls under Leo by virtue of its being invented by the first Frederick, who called his son Maximilian because he hoped he would combine the virtues of Fabius Maximus and Scipio Aemilianus, Romans he admired. Frederick is a Leo name; Frederick III was a Leonine king.

MIRABEL Now a girl's name; but originally a boy's (see page 42).

MORAG Mainly used in Ireland, from the Gaelic for 'the sun' which rules Leo.

MYLOR A Gaelic word meaning 'prince'; a place-name in Cornwall, and occasionally a christian name too.

NAPOLEON The name seems to have come from the Italian city of Naples; everyone now thinks of Buonaparte, though Frenchmen rarely used it. It is sometimes used in England. Napoleon himself was a quintessential Leo.

OLIVER The *olivier* or olive-tree is a Leo tree, and so the name belongs here. It has always been popular in England except for a generation after the death of Cromwell.

ORLANDO The Italian form of Roland (a Leo name; see below). Oddly enough, the first prominent Orlando, the hero of Shakespeare's *As You Like It*, was the son of a Rowland.

QUENTIN *Quinctus*, in Latin: 'fifth', and Leo is the fifth sign of the zodiac. The name was first popular around the town of St Quentin in France, where the saint was martyred in the third century; the Normans brought it to England.

REUBEN The Hebrew name for a boy taking the place of a son who has died; the idea of 'male-ness' is a Leo one.

REX Probably the plainest and best of Leo names (after Leo itself); meaning, of course, 'king'. Oddly, a very modern name.

RICHARD In the main, meaning 'ruler', and the name taken by a line of English kings; despite Richard III, a popular name, generally shortened to Dick (or, in past centuries, the charming 'Dickon').

RODERICK 'Famous ruler'; a name often used in Scotland, and occasionally elsewhere. Roderigo popular in Spain.

ROLAND Sometimes Rowland: the Old German 'fame' seems to place it under Leo. The name of the most famous nobleman of Charlemagne's court.

SAMPSON 'Sun-child' in Hebrew, so certainly Leo, for that sign is ruled by the sun. Occasionally spelt Samson, as was the famous Israelite warrior. A Welsh Samson travelled from Wales to Cornwall, then Brittany in the fifth century, and his name stayed.

STEPHEN A very common Greek name (borne by the first Christian martyr, in fact), Stephen means in the Greek, 'crown', which seems to place it firmly in Leo. Well known in England since the Norman Conquest.

THEODORIC 'Ruler of the people', in the Old German; the diminutive, Terry, is sometimes used as an independent name. See also, Derek (page 44).

ULRIC *Wulf ric*, in Old English, means wolf-ruler, which sounds a little Arian, but is certainly Leonine in feeling. Very occasionally found today.

VLADIMIR A Slavic name meaning 'glory of princes', with a regal Leonine ring about it. Popular in Russia, and brought to the west after the Revolution.

WALTER 'Rule the folk', says the Old German; a favourite Norman name which has been in use since the eleventh century in the English-speaking world.

XERXES The Persian for King.

ZEBEDEE 'Father', in Hebrew, says one authority; Leo is the father's sign.

YOUR LEO CHILD

If Charles or Augusta show you a painting they have done, say it's superb and tell them what good artists they are – they will go straight off and do another! Look at it in a destructive, critical way, and they will close their paintbox and may not produce another work of art for months! The Leo child thrives on encouragement – perhaps far more than any other type. Criticism must obviously be given, but for it to be accepted and acted upon it should be preceded by praise, and given constructively. It is the Leo enthusiasm for life and creativity that should really be nurtured, for it is a precious commodity, and will not only stand young Leo in good stead later in life, but at its best will communicate to all those with whom he comes into contact – both personally and professionally.

How to control all this exuberance? It isn't too easy without clouding the Leo sunshine; but the parents of Leo children have to take an extremely firm hand, so that exuberance doesn't become bumptiousness, and the joyful organisation of games and 'happenings' for friends, bossiness. These are the major Leo faults. 'I'm King of the Castle' might be sung to all intents and purposes in fun, but if young Leo's brothers and sisters believe it, so will Leo; and he will simply run the roost. Yes, he will do it extremely well – but royal magnanimity (for which the sign is renowned!) could all too easily become dictatorship.

Surprisingly, in all this, what is often not appreciated is that the Leo child (and adult for that matter) is far more sensitive than may be realised. When hurt, it is not usual for them to show it, in spite of their dramatic flair. They retire and, lion-like, lick their wounds; while they are forgiving by nature, such wounds can in point of fact take much longer to heal than appears the case.

The Leo child is creative, and somewhere in every Leo there is some kind of artistic creativity crying to come out; so paints and paper should be early acquisitions, and other forms of artistic expression should if possible be encouraged. Both sexes love to dance and act – school drama groups and ballet classes are an excellent idea. Although they like to look at and enjoy paintings and beautiful things (the girls will collect junk jewellery from the cradle – gradually 'converting' it to the real thing as soon as possible) they are 'doers'; they should be encouraged to *make*, and to fill their lives with as many activities as possible, or as can be afforded by the parents! It may well be that the crazes for various activities that so many children have are less likely to occur in Leos, for they are people who have long, passionate affairs rather than fleeting relationships – and this applies to interests as well as people. Young Leo, once hooked on a subject or interest, will probably carry it with him to the grave, and will strive for a high professional standard in whatever he does. Obviously, early training is going to be a greater influence on the life-pattern than it may well be for many types.

At school the Leo child should do extremely well, but will suffer a very great deal from any carping, over-critical teacher. Leo exuberance can be annoying to some people, and this is often a major source of set-back. They will not suffer fools gladly, but may have to learn to do so! If not given their heads, they can really crumble. They make excellent class-leaders, and want everything done 'properly', but have a big and generous attitude in general. They will get more pleasure from seeing their birthday parties being enjoyed by all their friends than in going to someone else's – for that is good ego-boosting stuff: there they are, Kings or Queens of their Castle! And they will not lack willing subjects.

Leo children are children of the Sun, and thrive most during the summer. They are usually strong and will always walk very well. Physical exercise, if it doesn't come through dancing or the usual sports activities at school, is more than necessary for them, as Leo rules the heart: Leos in good physical trim will be less likely to suffer from heart weaknesses. In winter they need to be kept particularly warm – most of them will gradually realise that the cold months of the year do not find them at their best!

VIRGO

23rd August–22nd September

VIRGO

GIRLS

AGNES The French, Italian, Spanish and Greek versions of the name all derive from the original Greek adjective meaning 'pure' and 'chaste' – primary Virgoan qualities. St Agnes was an archetypal Virgo, one of the most famous of all Roman martyrs, who refused to think of marriage, and had the simple lamb as her emblem. Unmarried girls celebrated her festival with particular enthusiasm; and for three centuries, up to 1700, here was one of the three most popular Christian names in England (in those days it was pronounced *Annis*). In Welsh it became the popular Una; and the enchanting pet-name Taggy was used for small Agneses.

ALBINA is an unusual Virgoan name, deriving from the Latin *albus*, 'white'. The great English Cecil family preserved it until fairly recently; when it is used today, it is usually as *Albinia*.

ALICE Most people associate the name with Lewis Carroll's marvellous fable *Alice in Wonderland*, and that Alice was so Virgoan in her qualities that she ensures its place on this page. It was a very common name in England and France as long ago as the twelfth century (as Alys); later it became 'old-fashioned', and was less used, until the publication of Mr Carroll's book revived it.

ALINE A charming, uncommon name thought to be derived from Alice; though it might come from *Adeline*, meaning 'noble', in which case it might be considered a Leo name.

AMELIA Virgoans never stop working, in one way or another (often on behalf of friends), so the fact that Amelia probably derives from the Old German word for 'labour' places them firmly here. When the Hanover family came to England and began to rule, Amelia became a popular name (though the British called George III's favourite daughter, Princess Amelia – Emily!).

ANCILLA An almost forgotten name, popular in the seventeenth century particularly in the English West Country. It comes from the Latin *ancilla*, 'handmaid'.

ATHENE The Greek goddess Athene presides over the city of Athens, always considered a Virgoan city. Never very common as a christian name, but those in search of mystery might like to experiment with a name for which no one has ever been successful in finding an origin!

BARBARA One of the four great virgin saints: a girl of great beauty, whose father shut her away in a tower out of the way of numerous suitors (so perhaps her virginity was less than completely willing). Her name was popular from the end of the twelfth century onwards, and was invoked as a protection against thunder and lightning (forced to put her to death, her father had been reduced to ashes by a sudden flash!). It shared the sudden burst of popularity many medieval names experienced early this century. 'Babs' is the pet-name.

BLANCHE from the French adjective 'white': pure, virginal. Blanch of Artois brought it to England when she came to marry the Earl of Lancaster in the thirteenth century. It went out of fashion in the nineteenth century, when it was considered 'old fashioned', but revived early this century.

BLODWEN A Welsh name: from *blod-yn* (flower) and *gwen* (white).

CARMEL The name of a Palestinian mountain dedicated, in its church and convent, to the Virgin, who in legend brought Jesus there. Carmen, in Spanish: but the heroine of the opera is about as un-Virgo as she could be.

CHARMIAN Shakespeare used the name for one of Cleopatra's slaves: her nobility shows that Virgos need not all be timid, and the origin of the name, in Plutarch, is the Greek for 'a little joy', which can be Virgo's lot. But 'to serve' is a Virgoan motto.

CLAUDIA The feminine form of Claud (see below). Occurring in the Bible, it was adopted in England in the late sixteenth century; in French, Claude. The Welsh Gladys is said to come from the same source.

CLOVER Virgoans love wild-flowers, of which clover is of course one.

CORA This seems to have originated in America, sometime in the last century: it is said to mean 'maiden', and if so is obviously Virgoan.

DONNA From the Italian *Madonna*, 'lady', with associations with the Virgin. Somewhat popularised recently by the song *Waiting for my Donna*, in *Hair*.

DORCAS 'A roe or gazelle' in Greek, but most associated with the Dorcas of the Acts of the Apostles, who made coats and clothes for the poor: a very Virgoan activity.

EMMELINE From the same root as Amelia (see above), Emmeline was introduced into England by the Normans; during the Middle Ages it sometimes became the pretty Emblen. The modern use of the name came with the late Stuarts.

FABIA The feminine version of Fabian (see page 54).

FRANCES From the same root as Francis (see page 54): many European countries have used the name in one form or another, and it has always been popular.

GLADYS A version of Claudia (see above), the name was first Welsh (Gwladys) – and must have led to much confusion, for Welsh Gladys's commonly signed themselves Claudia!

GWEN The pet-form of Gwendolyn (see below).

GWENDOLYN The Welsh 'white'. She was Merlin's wife in the *Vita Merlini* (there can rarely have been a dull moment, and one wonders how a Virgoan would cope!).

HAZEL Small bushes and trees are ruled by Mercury, so this plant name finds itself here rather than under Taurus. A modern name.

IDA From the Old Norse word for 'labour', and Virgos always think of themselves as (and generally are) immensely hard workers. The Normans brought the name to England.

INEZ From Agnes (see page 50).

JOYCE A popular name in medieval times, mainly because of the popularity of St Jodoc of St Josse-sur-Mer, whose cult spread right through France (a Virgoan country). Used as a man's name for some time, but recently only for a woman; now, quite popular again.

KOREN A Greek name, meaning 'young girl'.

LEE In the Old English, 'meadow'. The countryside connotation places it under Virgo.

LUCIA St Lucia (or Lucy, for the name is often spelt that way) is the patron saint associated with the sight; Mercury (which rules Virgo) rules the nervous system, so Lucy (a virgin martyr, too) perhaps belongs here. A favourite name in England from the seventeenth century on.

LUCINDA From Lucia (see above).

MALVA In the Gaelic, 'handmaiden'; Virgos love to serve.

MAMIE An American version of Mary (see below).

MANON French: from Mary (see below).

MARGERY Most scholars derive this name from the herb *marjoram*, ruled by Mercury (ruler of Virgo), which according to Culpeper 'strengthens the stomach' – a Virgoan area of the body!

MARIA The Italian, originally Latin, form of Mary (see below), often popular in England.

MARIE The French spelling of Mary (see below).

MARIETTA Marietta, Ohio, the American town, seems to be the original of this version of Mary (see below).

MARY Of course, from its association of the Virgin, *the* Virgo name (though its original meaning, in Hebrew, 'wished-for child', has no Virgo attributes). For some years the name was carefully guarded: but after the twelfth century it became more and more popular, until by the eighteenth century one-fifth of all girls born in England were christened Mary. Occasionally, Roman Catholics have called male children Mary, generally as a second name.

MAUREEN Irish version of Mary (see above), popular in the U.S.A.

MERCEDES A Spanish derivative from Mary (see above): its association recently with a make of motor car has limited its use in English-speaking countries, though it is still often used in France.

MILLICENT 'Strong worker', in Old German, which suggests a good Virgoan housemaid! Millie is now popular.

MINNIE In Scotland, originally a pet-name for Mary (see above).

MOIRA The Irish form of Mary (see above).

MOLLY Derived from Mary (see above).

NESSIE Really a derivative of Agnes (see above); not from Loch Ness, where the legendary monster has been called Nessie for a number of years, and might suggest an over-ambitious Scorpio!

PRUNELLA Latin: 'self-heal' – the name of a plant. Virgoans are good nurses and doctors, preoccupied with healing.

ROBERTA From Robert (see page 55).

SHAMA In Hebrew, 'obedient woman'; obviously a Virgoan!

SILVIA Now slightly old-fashioned, this charming name from the Latin *silvius*, 'a wood', suggests a Virgoan love of the country. Shakespeare used 'Silvius' as a man's name.

SUSAN Sometimes Susanna; the purity of the Susannah whose behaviour rebuked the Elders in the Apochrypha suggests Virgo (though her figure may have been more Taurean!).

TAGGET The charming, rather rustic pet-name for Agnes (see page 50).

TERESA Probably from the Greek for 'to reap', and harvesting generally is taken to fall under Virgo, in which sign the sun is when one reaps. St Teresa of Avila, the first woman to find a place among the doctors of the church, made the name popular; St Therese of Lisieux renewed its popularity, though it did not become really common in England until the eighteenth century. Thomas Hardy reduced it to Tess in his great novel.

TRINA In the Greek, 'pure'. Enough said.

VESTA The association with the Vestal Virgins suggests Virgo; though Vesta was the Roman goddess of fire, which as strongly suggests Leo!

VIRGINIA Undoubtedly Virgo: popular in France because of *Paul et Virginie*, Bernadin de St Pierre's novel, in which the heroine is Virgo to a lunatic degree; in America where the first child born of English parentage (in August, 1587) was christened Virginia after the Virgin Queen Elizabeth!

YVONNE One of the most popular of all French names; and because no derivation seems possible, placed here because Virgo rules France.

BOYS

BLASE An attractive name, the origins of which are obscure: but in Latin *blaesus* is 'splay-footed', and since Virgo has a remote connection with the lame god Vulcan, we have placed it here. As the patron saint of wool-workers, he might be said to have an Arian connection; but again, the occupation of weaving is a very Virgoan one. In medieval times, when the wool trade was so important in England, Blase became a popular name.

BRUNO From the Old German *brun*, brown – a Virgo colour. In England, it became the very common surname Brown, but Bruno is found occasionally, still, as a christian name.

CLAUDE Probably from *claudus*, 'lame', so under Virgo for the same reason as Blase (above). Came to England from France in 1543.

COSMO From the Greek for 'order', a very Virgoan attribute. Became a favourite name in Italy (sometimes as Cosimo), probably because of the martyr Kosmas; came first to Scotland, then to England, where it was used regularly until very recently it fell out of fashion.

DARCY A name which grew from that of a patch of land at Arcy-St-Restitue, in France; an earthy name which must surely fall under *the* earth sign.

DIGGORY From an ancient English romance, of *Sir Digore*, it seems to have been most used in Cornwall, and to have belonged mainly to servants (looked after by Virgo).

DEAN Popular particularly in America, the name comes from the Old English for 'valley', which makes it Virgoan by nature.

ELLIS Somehow, in the seventeenth century, the girl's name Alice (see above) became Ellis, and a boy's name.

ENOCH From the Hebrew word for 'trained', or 'skilled': Virgoans will take endless trouble in learning a skill or craft. Only came into use in the seventeenth century.

EPHRAIM Probably from the Hebrew, 'meadows'. Used sparingly in England in the seventeenth century; still used in the U.S.A.

FABIAN This romantic-sounding name, well used in the sixteenth century, probably derives from the Latin *faba*, 'a bean', and we place it under Virgo for this vegetable reason, though one must admit it sounds as though it belongs under a more flamboyant sign.

FRANCIS 'A Frenchman.' The name became popular after the cult of St Francis of Assisi spread throughout Europe in the thirteenth century. He got it because his father was nicknamed Francesco during a business trip to France. France is, of course, a Virgo country. Frank is the usual diminutive.

FRANK An abbreviation of Francis (see above), though it stood on its own from at least 1066 onwards.

GALAHAD Sir Lancelot's son, in the Arthurian legend: the pure and spotless knight who achieved the Holy Grail, and could scarcely have been anything but Virgoan. Tennyson made the name well-known (like the other names of the knights in the *Queste del' Saint Graal*) in his long and popular *Idylls of the King*, and for a time it was very popular in Victorian and Edwardian England.

GASTON A peculiarly French name, meaning 'from Gascony': a Virgoan part of a Virgoan country. Occasionally used in England.

GERVASE Sometimes spelt Gervais, the name comes from the Celtic for 'servant', and Virgoans have a high ideal of service. Well loved in the twelfth and thirteenth centuries, and still used in the English Elwes family, which has christened its sons Gervase since 1615.

KEVIN St Kevin, an Irish saint who popularised the name, had the typical Virgoan love of wild nature.

MAITLAND Old English 'of the plains'; the Virgoan loves wide-open country-side. Now substantially an American name.

MALCOLM In the Gaelic, 'servant' (originally, of the Church); Virgoans make good servants, which in modern parlance means they actually enjoy perform-ing tasks for others. Originally a Scottish name.

MALISE 'Servant of Jesus', in the Gaelic; see under Malcolm (above).

MARMADUKE This now unfashionable name was popular in hard-headed Yorkshire, and came from the Gaelic 'servant of Maedoc', Mr Maedoc being the lucky employer of a Virgoan serving-man. Sometimes used in America, but simplified to Duke.

NEWELL In the Latin, a kernel or nut-seed: nuts are governed by Virgo.

OSBERT Predominantly a French name (from Anosbert); and Virgo rules France. Fairly common in early centuries, now less so, Sir Osbert Sitwell being the most prominent man recently to bear it.

PERCIVAL 'Pierce the valley', in French, valleys always suggesting Virgo; Sir Perceval, one of the purest of King Arthur's knights, sounds Virgo also.

PERCY The name of a famous French family (Virgo rules France). At first, confined to that family; later popular (Shelley's christian name was Percy), but latterly for some reason considered effete.

ROBERT Predominantly a French name, brought over to England at the time of the Conquest, and reinforced by the old English name Hreodbeorht. Rob and Robin come from it. Here because Virgo rules France; though an Old German derivation, 'bright fame', might suggest Aries or even Leo.

RUPERT From the English Hreodbeorht (see Robert, above); no association seems to suggest an astrological compartment for the name, so we bracket it with its neighbour.

SHAW In Old English, 'from the grove', suggesting a Virgoan love of sylvan glades.

SILAS Seems to be a shortening of Silvanus, the god of trees, suggesting Virgo.

SILVESTER From the Latin, 'found in a wood', a natural place for a Virgoan to be found. St Silvester, a pope, cured the Emperor Constantine of leprosy, which seems to indicate a Virgoan love of medicine.

VANCE 'A thresher': associated with the harvest, which usually is reaped when the sun is in Virgo.

VERE A name derived from a famous family of Ver, in Normandy; there is no other derivation, so we place the name under the sign that rules France.

VERNON As with Vere, above, the association is with France, where it is a common place-name.

WARNER A folk-name from the Old German, and Virgo is perhaps the sign most associated with folk-legend.

YOUR VIRGO CHILD

The old adage 'If you want something done, ask a busy person' applies in no small way to the Virgoan child, and it is just because they are such useful members of the family to have around – to do an errand here, take a telephone message there – that parents have to be just a little careful they don't take advantage of the traditional role of Virgo: to serve. Interestingly, young Malcolm won't usually mind a bit, because he loves to run messages and use the telephone; but we think that it is important that in the execution of duty, *responsibility* should also be given, and quite a fair bit of it. While the Virgo child is a willing worker, confidence is needed, and knowing that he has responsibility to carry is an excellent way to build it. The parents of Virgo children must not, however, confuse responsibility with organisation, for Virgo is usually not a very good organiser; best tell them exactly what has to be done, and when – encouraging the writing of notes and lists if necessary – *then* leave it to them to carry on with the job in hand, giving much praise and if necessary some criticism when all is completed. The Virgoan trait to criticise is an interesting one, for Virgos do not mind being criticised in turn; they will not mind their mistakes being analysed in detail, and will as a result do much better next time.

The Virgo child will like to be extremely busy, but sometimes because of their variety of interests there is a tendency to 'run around in circles'. While they will eventually get somewhere, they may take a long time, and waste energy, on the way. This is, of course, due to lack of organising ability as opposed to lack of energy, which Virgoans have in plenty. The energy itself however is often of a rather highly-strung, nervous kind, and it is possible for Virgoan children (as well as adults) to become tense and live on their nerves. It is difficult for them to relax, and especially at examination-time at school worry and tension may easily cause sleeplessness and, more importantly, nervous tummy upsets. This is a Virgoan health hazard, and if upsets occur for no apparent reason, it is up to parents to question young Alice, and get her to explain in detail what has gone wrong, for the cause of the illness could well be worry. Virgoans are natural analysts, so the 'in depth' approach to school problems, getting the child to rationalise difficulties, is the best answer — then the tummy-ache will ease, probably overnight!

Young Virgo will love to have hobbies, and if there is a garden the nicest thing a parent can do is to 'give' a little plot, however small, to little Alice or Malcolm: then, as soon as nature permits, up will come the carefully arranged plants, and Virgo will realise that another attribute is green fingers. Virgoans love to 'find out', so school subjects involving research are often attractive. The scientific areas aligned to nature – botany, for instance – are likely to appeal very strongly. All work will be done very neatly and carefully: the Virgoan child's exercise book will look beautiful, filled with the neatest handwriting, and with hardly a smudgy mark in sight. In many ways the Virgo child can become the teacher's pet, because of the willingness to work, to tidy away books after school, to be careful and methodical and systematic, and to take orders and carry them out.

One of the best forms of exercise for Virgoan children is cycling. They love the outdoors, and are basically at their best in the country. Long walks will appeal tremendously.

Because Virgoans are perfectionists, they tend to expect perfection in others, and if they do not get it they can all too easily be over-critical. If this rather negative trait is not controlled by parents, it can have rather a bad effect on their emotional relationships in later life. Should the tiny Virgoan begin to criticise his friends severely, it must be pointed out that too few people are perfect, and that faults must be accepted in others — as the parents have to accept young Virgo's! The emotional level in many Virgoans is not terribly high, and it is just possible that they may rationalise feelings away ('It's silly to feel like that about it!'). Again this is an area that needs direction, for a tendency to inhibit the more emotional areas of the personality can make them seem remote or indeed 'virginal' to others.

LIBRA

23rd September–22nd October

LIBRA

GIRLS

AMABEL The Latin adjective 'lovable' is *amabilis*: what could be more Libran? It became the far less beautiful *Mabel* (it also became *Amable* and *Amiable*!), and was used a great deal in Victorian three-volume sentimental novels.

AMANDA 'Fit to be loved', in the Latin, and invented in the seventeenth century.

AMY From the Old French *Amée*, or the modern *aimée*, from the verb *aimer*, to love. Amy Robsart, the tragic wife of the Earl of Leicester, in Elizabethan England, helped to popularise the name. Sir Walter Scott used it in *Kenilworth*, one of his most famous novels, and this started a revival, particularly in Scotland.

ANNABELLA Probably derives from *Amabel* (see above), and popular in Scotland, and later in England. Edgar Alan Poe's poem *Annabel Lee* helped to popularise it for a while in America, later in Europe.

CELIA No apparent 'meaning': we place it here because Shakespeare used it for Rosalind's friend in *As You Like It*, a Libran heroine if ever there was one!

CLARIBEL Found in Shakespeare's *Tempest*: he may have originated the name. Some authorities say it means 'bright, shining, beautiful' – all Venus attributes, and Venus rules Libra.

DESDEMONA A particularly beautiful name for a Libran, for it comes from the Shakespearean play *Othello*, and Desdemona there is the very best kind of Libran: utterly honest, utterly faithful, seeking to do good even when it is dangerous for her. In Verdi's opera, pronounced Desdémona, which is perhaps more beautiful than the common Desdemona.

CHERYL An Old English name, now much used in America: meaning, simply, 'love' – and Libra is perhaps the most loving of the signs.

EDNA In the Hebrew, the name seems to mean 'delight', which has a Libran ring about it. It can only be traced to 1860 as a modern christian name, though the original Edna was Enoch's wife, in the Apocrypha.

FELICIA Seems to have appeared as the female of Felix (see page 60).

FELICITY Derived also from Felix (see below), and more common than Felicia. Used in England in the seventeenth century, when the puritans began using many nouns as christian names.

HAIDÉE From the Greek 'to caress', which is Libran in tone, and matches well with the description of the long kiss exchanged by the most famous Haidée and her lover, in Byron's *Don Juan*, which made the name famous for a generation.

HEPZIBAH 'My delight is in her', is the translation of the Hebrew; very Libran description! Used perhaps chiefly in America since the seventeenth century, but also in the English West Country.

IRENE 'Peace', in Greek; the name came first to England in 1880, and John Galsworthy made it well known by using it in *The Forsyte Saga*. Sometimes, the ugly Renie is used.

ISADORA The female version of Isadore (see page 61).

JASMIN It is difficult to deny Jasmin, with its ineffable sweetness, a place under Libra. In Persian, the name means 'fragrant flower'. It became briefly popular in England after the spectacular production of Flecker's *Hassan*, in 1923.

JOLETTA A derivative from viola, the pansy, or love-in-idleness, which seems to paint a thumbnail sketch of a loving Libran!

JOY A christian name since the twelfth century: the Libran loves to be joyful and happy.

JUSTINA See Justin (page 61).

KATHERINE A virgin martyr, St Katherine took her name from the Greek for 'pure', which suggests Libra rather than Virgo. The name (sometimes as Catherine) seems to have been brought back to England by the Crusaders from the Middle East, where she was celebrated as the lady who declined to be crucified on a (catherine-)wheel – it fell to pieces, and several lookers-on were killed by splinters. Kate, Kitty, Cathy and Kay are pet-names derived from Katherine. Kathleen and Katrine also come from it.

KETURAH Sometimes found in America, the name from the Hebrew 'fragrance' suggests the delicacy of Libra.

LOVEDAY A charming Cornish name, originally popular throughout England; it has a very Libran derivation – a 'love-day' was a day on which two people would appoint a meeting to resolve a difference or end a quarrel!

MABEL A version of Amabel (see page 58), now far more popular than its prettier original.

MELODY A Libran will love tuneful music!

MILDRED From the Old English for 'mild strength' – Librans, mild-mannered enough, can be much firmer than one thinks! St Mildred, an English martyr, 'a comforter to all in affliction', made the name popular from the ninth century on.

MIRANDA Shakespeare invented the name for his character in *The Tempest*, 'admired Miranda' – and the name seems to stem from the Latin *miranda*, 'admired', which will suit most typical Librans.

PATIENCE Simply from the noun: and most Librans like to 'wait and see what happens' before deciding on a course of action. E. G. Withycombe (in the *Oxford Dictionary of English Christian Names*) reminds us that a former Speaker of the House of Commons named his daughters Patience, Temperance, Silence and Prudence, though he does not reveal whether they lived up to them.

PHILOMENA In the Greek, 'I am loved' – the ambition of all Librans.

QUERIDA From the Spanish, 'I am loved'.

RUTH An uncertain derivation of this name suggests that it originated from the Hebrew 'beauty': Venus, the planet of beauty, rules Libra.

SAMANTHA From the American Indian, 'lovely flower'.

SELMA Popular especially in the U.S.A., the name appears to have originated in Scotland, and to stem from the Gaelic for 'fair'. Librans are usually this, in one way or another.

SHEILA Originally from Celia (see page 58), and originally an Irish version, though now common in other countries too.

SHIRLEY A surname commonly used as a christian name, it first appeared in Charlotte Brontë's novel *Shirley* in 1849; it became common both in America and England during the 1930s, because of the stardom of Shirley Temple; and as she is a Libran, we place it here in tribute to her!

SORRELL The herb sorrel, from which the name is taken, is ruled by Venus; Venus rules both Taurus and Libra. But sorrel is used, in herbalism, to cool inflammation of the blood. Arians suffer, often, from 'hot-bloodedness' of various kinds, and this is the opposite sign to Libra – so we place Sorrell under the latter sign, rather than Taurus. (One of the more technical astrological name-placings!).

VENETIA Though some authorities believe the name to be an English version of Gwenyth, it seems much more likely to be derived from Venice, a Libran city.

VIDA In Hebrew, 'beloved' – and Librans love to be loved.

ZENA 'Hospitable' in Greek; Librans can offer legendary hospitality.

ZILLAH In Hebrew, 'shade': Librans will always be happiest in shady circumstances, rather than in too much blazing sun!

BOYS

ALAN Alan, Allan, or Allen seems to derive from an ancient Celtic expression for 'harmony' – certainly a Libran conception. *Alain* Férgeant brought it over to England with William the Conqueror, and it travelled north to Scotland, where it became extremely popular (as popular as Alain still is in Brittany). Alan is the most usual English form.

AMYAS The possibility that this name derived from the girl's name *Amy* suggests that it should be Libran: Camden, the historian, wrote in 1605 that 'we do now use Amias in difference from Amie the woman's name'. It was not until Charles Kingsley used the name for the hero of his famous *Westward Ho!* that it became popular in England, and then unfortunately only briefly.

CAILLIN Welsh: 'peace-maker', and obviously Libran.

CLIVE The surname of Robert Clive, the Libran Englishman so connected with India; used as a christian name by those associated with that country, but now generally common, partly because of the novelist Thackeray, who started the fashion in *The Newcomes* (1855).

DARBY A popular form of Diarmid (see below): Darby and Joan, as a symbol of married bliss, originated in a poem published in *The Gentleman's Magazine* in 1735.

DEMPSTER A form of Diarmid (see below).

DIARMID Diarmid, or Diarmit, Diarmuit or Dermot, are all from the Old Irish *di-fharmait*, 'free from envy'. Librans are certainly not usually envious.

FAUSTUS The Latin, *faustus*, means 'fortunate', and Librans can certainly be that; the Faust legend suggests a less happy being, though, with the Libran tendency to hanker after the unattainable. Used generally in Italy and Germany.

FELIX In the Latin, 'happy'. Four Popes and one or two saints were called Felix, and the name was popular in the Middle Ages; more recently suggesting often a name for a cat rather than a human. The name is used today, however.

FERGUS The Old Celtic word is *gustus*, or choice, implying the making of a decision and the balancing of preferences. Scottish and Irish mainly, but sometimes used in England.

GEOFFREY Libran peacemakers are suited by this name, which contains the Old French word *frithu*, or 'peace'. Common in the twelfth to the fifteenth centuries, then unpopular, and now thoroughly back in favour.

HUMPHREY Sometimes spelt without the 'e', Humphrey comes from the Old English word for 'peace', which a Libran will crave. A very popular Middle Ages name, then spelt Humfrey.

ISADORE Part of the original Greek means 'a gift', so the name can be placed under Libra; Librans are free with gifts. Isadora is the female form. Perhaps chiefly, in modern times, a Jewish name.

JUSTIN From the Latin, 'just', which suggests justice with her Libran scales. Sagittarius no doubt has a claim, however. Two Byzantine emperors possessed the name, which gave it an impetus. Popular, still, in Ireland; in England it has tended to become a surname.

JUSTINIAN From the same root as Justin (see above).

KYLE In the Gaelic, 'fair' or 'handsome'. . .

LOVELL Originally, from the simple 'love', above all a Libran aspiration and desire. Has now become a surname, too.

MANFRED 'Man of peace' in the Old German; came to England with the Normans. Occasionally used at the end of the nineteenth century, as a result of Byron's poem of that name.

MEREDITH A name still popular in Wales, where it originated: one etymologist says 'brought together without mixing', which has perhaps Libran overtones.

NATHAN A predominantly Jewish name, from the Hebrew for 'gift': Librans are certainly loving *and* giving.

SEPTIMUS 'Seventh', in Latin; Libra is of course the seventh sign of the zodiac. The name was quite popular in Victorian England.

YOUR LIBRA CHILD

Think of Libra and one at once thinks of natural charm – and a very great deal of it. Certainly most Librans have an above-average share of this, and it makes its presence felt from the earliest age. It is extremely easy to spoil Libran children, because they are charming and delightful and pick up politeness and good habits as easily as many other types pick up bad ones! However, because of all this Libra may soon find out that a winning smile and a big 'thank-you' will attract all life's goodies on a plate: or so they may think. Parents, beware! Some fairly strict character-building is necessary, even if it is hard to administer, because the 'getting-away-with-murder' charm can lead to weakness, and it is strength of character which develops the best expression of Libran charm – not too gushing.

It is all-important for the parents of Libran children to start training them to make their own decisions. This really can be a terrible stumbling-block for the

Libran, and periods of decision will simply be lived through until they are forced to resolve the problems – or the problems become no longer relevant! It is good for young Ruth to decide which colour hair-band she is going to buy, and not to have to go to mother for a final decision. Certainly mother can make suggestions ('If you have the blue one, it will match your blue-and-pink dress; if the red, you can wear it with your jeans'), but however appealingly she is looked to, she should *only* reassure her daughter, and put the various possibilities sympathetically. This is all-important, and fully to be recommended to all parents of Libran children. Do *not* make decisions for them!

Perhaps the worst Libran fault is resentfulness, and this must be watched for. Young Justin may complain 'I gave *him* that toy car, and he's only sent *me* a birthday card!' Precisely the Libran attitude! Careful explanations are necessary before they get too upset in such situations.

It is 'getting upset', in fact, that is the Libran idea of hell. The children need a pleasant, balanced life, and domestic rows will upset them very badly, psychologically. They are surprisingly intuitive, so any family arguments – even if they do not actually overhear them – will be sensed, and they may develop headaches as a result. Headaches and slight kidney upsets are Libran health hazards, and sometimes the two are connected – an above-average number of headaches could be caused by disturbances in the kidneys.

The Libran at school will work beautifully at subjects that interest them – but boredom will lead to periods of drifting, and thinking about things that *do* interest them! A teacher will be likely to attribute this 'cutting out' to laziness, but that is not really the case – it will more than likely be the fault of the teacher, who is being boring! Music is to be encouraged in all young Librans. Often this is simply appreciative, but any indication of a desire to learn the piano or perhaps a string or woodwind instrument should very definitely be encouraged. The girls, being extremely fashion-conscious, will like to sew, and should be allowed to do so – choosing the fabric for themselves of course!

One of the most deeply-rooted psychological needs of any Libran is to find a partner. Some will, in spite of indecisiveness in other spheres of their lives, rush into emotional relationships, and may well learn the hard way. But in learning they will realise that they are not really psychologically whole until they can relate to their own loved one. As Libran children begin to grow up, the romantic scene could catch up with them at an early age, and they need help and an above-average amount of guidance. The girls, especially, will see their loves through rose-coloured spectacles, and while we would hate to spoil the fun by breaking those delicate instruments, we suggest to parents that they firmly point out to young Ruth that reality can bear little resemblance to fairy-tale, and that she should realise this – even if, at the time, she is deeply involved in the affair between Scarlett and Rhett, and identifying with them all the way!

So with young Librans – as with older ones – it must be balance and harmony all the way, and for their development we recommend an iron hand very carefully padded by a velvet glove.

SCORPIO

23rd October–21st November

SCORPIO

GIRLS

ANTONIA Sometimes *Antoinette*, this name comes from the boy's name Antony, certainly a Scorpio name.

AVIS Avis or Avice was formerly mainly a gypsy name, and gypsies always seem to be following a generally rather Scorpionic ideal. The name, never widely popular, has been around, in Europe, since the Norman times.

BATHSHEBA From the Hebrew, 'voluptuous'. In the Bible, the wife of Uriah and afterwards David, and the fashion for Biblican names popularised it for a few centuries. Another meaning is 'daughter of satiety', which seems not altogether un-Scorpionic!

BELINDA The Old German *lindi*, 'a snake', contributes to the name, which must belong here. Originally in the old romances, it did not become popular until Pope used it for the heroine of his poem *The Rape of the Lock*, and Purcell in his opera *Dido and Aeneas*; it remained rather literary (Maria Edgeworth's very popular novel *Belinda*, in 1801, helped to make it popular). Not very common today.

BRYONY 'Strong.' Scorpio is the strongest sign of the Zodiac, and also often prickly and emotional!

CLODAGH An attractive Irish name, and the name of a river in Tipperary; Scorpio is a water sign, more attached to the river than the sea.

DENISE 'Of Dionysia' – god of wine; and, yes, Scorpios generally like their glass or two. *Not* from the male Denis.

DÉSIRÉE From the French and Latin, 'desired' – what every Scorpio would wish to be!

DORINDA Modelled on Belinda (see above).

EGLENTYNE From a Latin word meaning 'prickly', and a name for the sweet-briar, both of which indicate Scorpio. Sometimes spelt Eglentine in England, it was revived for a while in Victorian times, but now seems sadly neglected.

ELFREDA 'Strength', in Old English; Scorpio is the strongest sign in the Zodiac. The original Elfreda was Mrs Ethelred-the-Unready. The name was revived by the Victorians.

ETHELINDA Nothing to do with 'Ethel' (a Cancerian name); from the Old German *athal lindi,* or noble serpent, so obviously a Scorpio.

GABRIELLE The feminine of Gabriel (see page 67).

GAENOR A derivative of Guinevere (see below).

GERTRUDE The Old German *strong spear* seems Scorpionic enough, and so does Queen Gertrude in *Hamlet*! Two St Gertrudes helped to make the name popular. In the Victorian age, 'Gertie' took over.

GYTHA A Norse name meaning 'war': aggressive enough for any Scorpio.

GUINEVERE The wife of King Arthur, who for her passion for Sir Lancelot and her betrayal of her husband seems to merit a Scorpio listing. Gaenor is a version sometimes used in Wales. In Cornwall, the name became Jennifer (see below).

HEDDA A Scandinavian name, meaning 'war'; but Hedda Gabler, Ibsen's famous heroine, seems Scorpionic, too.

HEDWIG Old German: 'strife, battle'.

ISMENA Often a gypsy name, and the gypsies seem often to have Scorpionic characters; used in Ireland until the end of the seventeenth century.

JANE In a roundabout version, derived from John, via Joan. So see under John, below. Jane was very common in the eighteenth and nineteenth century, and many lovers of Miss Austen must have christened daughters after her. Became rather 'lower-class' in Victorian years, but now, if anything, rather prestigious!

JANET A diminutive of Jane, see above; became very popular in Scotland, occasionally as Jennet. Popular in this century.

JEAN Yet another of the 'John' derivatives, and at first mainly used in Scotland; it probably arrived there as the French Jehane, in Bonnie Prince Charlie's time.

JENNIFER See Guinevere. (See above.)

JESSIE A Scottish version of Janet, a diminutive of Jane, derived from Joan, which comes from John! So, see under John, page 67.

JOAN Though Jane, Janet, Jean and Jessie are all popular, Joan is probably still the most common derivative of John (see page 67). St Joan of course gave the name enormous impetus, and by the sixteenth century it was the third most common girl's name in England. Perhaps for this very reason, it was then regarded as 'common' for some time, but today is as popular as ever.

JOANNA The last of the 'versions' of John, via Joan; it had the added reason for popularity of appearing in the Bible (as one of the women who tended Jesus).

LAVINIA A favourite gypsy name, and Scorpio rules gypsies and their lives. Originally a Roman name, which came into use in England fairly lately (eighteenth century).

LORELEI In Old German, the name of the water-nymphs who lured travellers to their deaths in the Rhine: Piscean influences, no doubt, but they must surely have been Scorpio girls?

MAGDALEN Sometimes Madeline, but in any event from the Mary Magdalen whose Scorpionic predelictions did not prevent Christ accepting her as a follower.

MAGDA The German version of Magdalen (see above).

MIRIAM In the Hebrew, 'the desired', which seems to hint at a Scorpio girl! Some etymologists have suggested the name comes from *meri*, 'rebellion', which would fit just as well. A favourite Jewish name, but now commonly used by Christians.

NETTA Or Nettie: Scottish versions of Janet (see above).

NITA Popular in the U.S.A., Nita is an abbreviation of the Spanish Juanita, itself a version of Joan (see above).

OCTAVIA Feminine of Octavius, or 'eighth'; Scorpio is the eighth sign.

OPAL The opal is a Scorpio stone.

SALOME Though the name comes from the Aramaic 'peace of Zion', the association with the seductive dancing daughter of Herodias (it was a favourite name with the Herods) is so Scorpionic that we place it here rather than under Libra.

SHENA The Gaelic version of Jane (see above).

WILLA The Old English for 'desirable', which is a Scorpionic concept in all sorts of ways!

ZITA The Celtic word for 'enticing', which sounds Scorpionic.

ZOË If Bernard Shaw was thinking of Scorpio when he coined the term 'the Life Force' for sex, then Zoë, which means 'life' in Greek, and was used as the Jewish equivalent of Eve, fits.

BOYS

ANTONY Antony or Anthony was the patron saint to whom one turned when one wanted to find something that had been lost; Scorpio gives one a capacity for meticulous searching, for discovery. The origin of the name is unknown, but the earliest famous Antony was Marcus Antonius, Caesar's friend. St Antony helped make the name popular during Christian times, and it has remained so. The 'h' only appeared in the name fairly recently, and was never meant to be pronounced, though lately in America it has been sounded. Tony is the popular pet-name.

AQUILA The Latin for *eagle* became popular in seventeenth-century England, mainly for men, though also for women.

ARNOLD No hesitation at all in filing this name under Scorpio, for it derives from the Old German *arenvald*, or 'a powerful eagle'. The Normans brought it to England, and though it fell out of favour for a while after the fifteenth century, more recently it has been used again.

BARRY The Irish word *bearrach* meant 'spear', a very Scorpionic weapon. Until the turn of the century only known in Ireland, but now increasingly popular in Britain and the U.S.A.

CYRIL The Greek word suggests a very autocratic 'lord and master', and the Scorpio rules far more strictly than the noble Leo! Both St Cyrils were doctors, and made the name known in Europe; it did not become common in England until the nineteenth century, and remains so.

DESMOND A name which originally described a man from Munster, used first in Ireland: but also perhaps from the Celtic for 'man of the world', suggesting Scorpion sophistication.

ERASMUS The Greek word is 'desired', which suggests Scorpio, even if the great scholar Desiderius Erasmus seems a mite desiccated for such a sensual origin. In the Middle Ages the christian name was well used in Eastern Europe, and was hereditary in the Darwin family (Erasmus was the grandfather of Charles).

EVAN The Welsh form of John (see page 67).

FERDINAND Bold and adventurous Scorpions match well with this name, a marriage of the Old German *fardi* (journey) and *nanthi* (risk). A very popular name in Spain and Italy, and used in France and England until the fourteenth century.

GABRIEL The strongest sign in the Zodiac seems the place for a name meaning 'God is a strong man', in the Hebrew.

HANS See John, below, from which it derives.

HERMAN 'An army man' in Old German; many Scorpios make a career in the Army, and the positions of planets in Scorpio often encourage them to high office. More popular in Germany, the name is still occasionally used in English-speaking countries, and emigrants made it mildly popular in the U.S.A.

HILDEBRAND *Hildi branda*, or 'battle-sword' in Old German; more enthusiastically warlike than an Arian, a Hildebrand seems Scorpion in inclination. St Hildebrand popularised the name (he was Pope Gregory VII, a great medieval pope).

HYMAN The masculine of 'Eve' — characteristic of the life force itself, and therefore Scorpionic, though dear immortal Hyman Kaplan could not be less Scorpio if he tried!

IAN Derived from John (see below).

JACK The commonest popular form of John, see below. Recently, boys have been christened 'Jack' without reference to the proper name of which it started as a version.

JAN A popular, rather rural form of John, popular especially in the English West Country.

JOHN The apostle's symbol, in art, is an eagle; the Scorpio symbols are an eagle and a scorpion. If the evidence of the Book of Revelation is taken into consideration, there seems to have been more than a touch of the Scorpionic imagination in the great apostle and evangelist. At first merely the most common of all Jewish names, by the eighteenth century a quarter of the male population of England was called John! It has been equally popular abroad.

JORDAN From the Hebrew, 'flowing down'; and Scorpio is perhaps the predominant water sign. From the twelfth century onward, many Englishmen took the name of the great river, and it was popular in particular with the puritans. The crusaders brought back the water of the Jordan to baptise little Jordans of their own. Recently, less popular, though used still in America.

KIERON In the Celtic, 'dark', suggesting Scorpio rather than Capricorn (though this is a personal inclination).

MAURICE 'A Moor', in the Latin, and Morocco is ruled by Scorpio. The name has been used in England since the twelfth century, originally spelt Morris.

OCTAVIUS In Latin, 'eighth', and Scorpio is the eighth sign of the zodiac. The famous Roman family (the Emperor Augustus was one of them) made the name popular in Italy; it was sometimes used in England for eighth children, but both these and the name are now rare.

OSWALD 'A powerful god', in the Old English; St Oswalds lived in England in the seventh and tenth centuries, the first at least (a Northumbrian king) being a doughty fighter. But the name is here because Scorpios really delight in power.

SEAN Irish for John (see above).

SHANE Americanised version of Sean (which is pronounced Shawn).

TONY See Anthony (page 66).

VIRGIL In the Latin, 'strong, flourishing'; Scorpio is the strongest of all signs.

VITALIS A name quite often used in England in the thirteenth and fourteenth centuries, if infrequently since; it means, in the Latin, 'life' or 'vitality' – and Scorpios have a most intense vitality.

ZANE A version of John (see page 67).

YOUR SCORPIO CHILD

The Scorpio qualities of determination, emotional strength and intensity will very soon begin to make their presence felt in the young Scorpio. Because they are such strong characters, they need very careful upbringing, and guidance from their parents – who, in order that these traits develop positively, must not hesitate to discipline them quite strictly if it is at all necessary. It is very necessary indeed for parents to explain their actions and the reasons for them, all along the way, for it is only thus that young Scorpios will understand their elders' motivations. If parents try to gloss over facts, the children will fill in those gaps for themselves, and having vivid imaginations will conjure up all sorts of reasons of their own. So in-depth explanations of why they should or should not do things is absolutely essential. This is also terribly important if, for instance, parents have to make changes in their own lives: perhaps having to go away, leaving young Denise or Barry behind. If they don't know exactly what is going on, they will think they are being plotted against or deserted – and this is not a good thing for them. They tend to be naturally secretive, and this will increase the tendency in a possibly negative way. To avoid this trait being negative, it can be developed consciously, and the ideal way is by letting the children plan surprises for the rest of the family at birthdays or Christmas and so on – in this way they can *enjoy* a bit of plotting and scheming on the side, without being underhand or sneaky (which can happen from time to time with this type).

   The emotional content of Scorpio is perhaps the highest of any of the twelve types. It is a marvellous force, but here again needs a lot of really positive direction. Soon, young Scorpio will begin to feel very strongly about certain issues. This is excellent, and all encouragement should be given to turn *feelings* into *actions*. It may be necessary to make them feel strongly about some issue, and help to remedy it: perhaps there is a rather lonely elderly person who would enjoy some visits from a child, or someone who cannot get out to shop or tidy the garden. Positive action derived from feeling is really excellent for young Scorpio.

The worst Scorpio fault is jealousy, and it is not an easy one for any Scorpio to come to terms with. It can cause difficulties early in life, when a young brother or sister arrives; and we think the only thing for parents to do is immediately to appeal to the Scorpio energy (both physical and emotional energy really are forces to be reckoned with), and get them to help out. Learning about the coming arrival during mother's pregnancy, listening to the baby's heart through Mummy's tummy, would help a very great deal, and if parents think that Scorpio is perhaps a little too young to cope with much information about 'where babies come from', they can think again; normally, add a good three years to Scorpio's age, and you will be about right in gauging their ability to cope with such complexities!

If all these very powerful Scorpio traits are harnessed, disciplined and directed, Scorpios can do very well at school. To 'know' in depth and detail, and to enjoy finding out 'why', is a basic motivation for them. The ability and energy to work hard is also present. Sport should be thoroughly enjoyed, and the tougher the sport the more attractive it will be, in many cases. Scorpios should learn to swim, as early as possible: this could lead to underwater swimming and diving and to water sports. The girls should enjoy judo, the boys boxing. A touch of cruelty is to be watched for: enjoyment of dissection in biology might be expressive! Usually there is a good business sense; Scorpios can make good butchers (or, more refinedly, good surgeons!), and researchers of all kinds. So subjects that could help towards careers of that sort are to be encouraged.

Scorpios often sing very well. They love all mystery stories (supernatural, horror or crime). Encouragement to write is often an excellent thing, expressing the powerful imagination, depth and intensity of this type in a positive and creative way – which is all-important.

SAGITTARIUS

22nd November–21st December

GIRLS

ALETHEA The Greek word for 'truth', a paramount Sagittarian concern, suggested this name, and when the Spanish Princess Maria Alethea came a-wooing Charles I (when he was Prince of Wales), it became popular in England. *Althea*, which it became later, perhaps falls more easily on the ear.

AUDREY A Sagittarian by courtesy of Shakespeare, who made the name famous as that of the rough, bawdy Sagittarian country girl in *As You Like It*. Actually, it had been around in strange forms (Aethelthryth, Awdrie, and so on) much earlier. Shakespeare probably chose it for its association with the word *tawdry*, describing the cheap necklaces sold at St Etheldreda's Fairs.

CANDIDA From the Latin, 'white'; but we look towards the heroine of Bernard Shaw's play, a real portrait of a straightforward, honest Sagittarian. It was Shaw who repopularised the name in England at the end of the last century.

CASSANDRA Cassandra was the daughter of Priam and Hecuba, and startled Troy by the accuracy of her prophesies; her foresighted wisdom suggests Sagittarius. A common name in England from the thirteenth century: Jane Austen had a sister Cassandra.

CLARA The Latin equivalent, 'bright' and 'clear' suggests the firey aspect of Sagittarius. St Clare of Assisi, the founder of the Poor Clares, made the name popular. Clare is perhaps the most often used form of the name, nowadays.

CORDELIA The daughter of King Lear who, by her honesty, caused the rift with her father with which Shakespeare starts his play. The name has occasionally been used since the seventeenth century, but not too often.

DANIELA From Daniel (see page 74).

DILYS The modern Welsh *dilys* means 'certainty', 'genuine'. Both Sagittarian qualities. The name was first used in Wales, but now has spread into England.

DINAH In the Hebrew, 'law suit', which suggests the lawyers' sign. A favourite name in working-class Victorian England (see the song *Willikins and his Dinah*).

ELIZABETH While the great Queen Elizabeth was a virgin queen, and might seem to give the name a Virgoan influence, she also had Sagittarius as her rising-sign, and the whole feeling of the Elizabethan Age is predominantly Sagittarian, with the long voyages of discovery, the comparative freedom to worship after the purges of Bloody Mary. The origin of the name is actually in the Hebrew *Elishba*, 'my God is satisfaction'. It came to England via Russia, Germany, Holland and France (as Isabel), and became popular in England at the end of the fifteenth century. By 1600, near the end of Elizabeth's reign, over 20% of girls were being christened by that name, in England. From it come Eliza, Betty, Betsie, Lizzie, Tetty, Elspeth, Elsie, Libby and Tibby.

ENA In the Old Irish, 'fire': Sagittarius is a fire sign. The name of a Queen of Spain, a Sagittarian country.

EUPHEMIA 'Auspicious speech', in the Greek, which certainly suggests Sagittarius; it was briefly fashionable in Victorian England.

FILIPA See Philippa (below).

HEATHER The kind of countryside associated with the plant which originated this name is especially Sagittarian: wide open windy country.

HIPPOLYTA Queen of the Amazons, which sounds thoroughly Sagittarian even if the name did not derive from Hippolytus, also of that sign (see below). Shakespeare was responsible for its popularity in Elizabethan times, and it has had a small vogue since.

HOPE Sagittarian optimism colours this name – used often in the seventeenth century, often for the sister of Faith and Charity.

HYACINTH Purple is a Sagittarian colour. St Hyacinth was a Roman martyr, so purple of mourning will suit him, too. Occasionally used as a man's name, until very recently.

IANTHE Shelley called his daughter Ianthe, and presumably got the name from a play, *The Siege of Rhodes* (where it rhymes, strangely, with 'dainty'). In Greek, 'violet flower', and violet is a Sagittarian colour. A pretty name, now virtually vanished.

INGRID The 'mounted heroine' of old Norway can only be Sagittarian.

ISA From Isobel (see below): chiefly Scottish.

ISOBEL Sometimes, too, Isabella, and a form of Elizabeth (see page 71). The Spaniards always used the name for the great Queen their king went a-wooing, and for centuries the names were interchangeable.

JACINTH The name derives from the Greek for hyacinth, a Sagittarian flower.

LILIAN Originally derived from Elizabeth (see above), and found independently in England after the nineteenth century. Lilibet was invented by Queen Elizabeth II, for herself, from the same source, when she was a small child.

LISETTE In the main, a French name which derives from Elizabeth (see page 71).

LORETTA A popular Roman Catholic name: Loreto, in Italy, was a popular place of pilgrimage; Sagittarius rules long and arduous journeys.

MINERVA Goddess of Wisdom; Sagittarius is the most sage of all the signs.

MONICA St Augustine's mother made the name known: ambitious for her son and rejoicing in his success, sometimes rather trying as a mother because of her high expectations, she sounds Sagittarian!

NONA From *nonus*, or ninth (in Latin); Sagittarius is the ninth sign of the zodiac.

PHILIPPA Sometimes spelt Phillipa, the name derives from Philip (see below), and is recorded as early as the fifteenth century (before that time, women were also called Philip). Pippa is an Italian form used by Browning in *Pippa Passes*.

PORTIA The derivation being uncertain, one connects the name with its most famous user – the heroine of Shakespeare's *Merchant of Venice*, who is as Sagittarian as any woman could hope to be.

RADEGUND 'Councillor of war'; suggesting an Arian Old German lady, but the emphasis on wisdom suggests too a Sagittarian, and St Radegund dealt so sensibly with her outrageous husband King Chlotar that one feels she may have been one. The name was used for both sexes, but most commonly for girls.

RONANNI A name invented by a young friend of the authors, for his baby sister, who is a Sagittarian.

ROSALIND Not only does the name stem from the Old German for 'horse', but Shakespeare used it in *As You Like It* for the most Sagittarian of all his characters (not even excepting Portia, see above).

ROSAMUND We have placed this name under Cancer; but part of its derivation from *hros*, the Old German for 'horse' (like Rosalind) does also suggest Sagittarius.

ROSE Though placed under Taurus the 'horse' derivation (as in Rosamund and Rosalind) also suggests Sagittarius, the half-horse human.

SCHOLASTICA Now thoroughly out-of-date, but also thoroughly Sagittarian, for it derives from the Latin for 'scholar'.

SONIA The Russian diminutive of Sophia (see below), which has been used in England since 1920.

SOPHIA From the Greek, 'wisdom', – a Sagittarian quality. Used in England since the eighteenth century, sometimes as Sophie. We do not necessarily suggest Miss Tucker as the complete Sagittarian!

VIOLA From the violet, a Sagittarian flower. Shakespeare's use of the name in *Twelfth Night* popularised it.

YOLANDE Derived from Viola (see above).

BOYS

AIDAN An Irish derivation, from *aid* – 'fire'; Sagittarius is a fiery sign, and one of the earliest Aidans was a monk and teacher at Lindisfarne – a Sagittarian profession.

ALFRED *Ealdfrith*, meaning 'great peace' in Old English, suggests a Sagittarian, though no one knows the astrological personality of Alfred the Great. This Christian name became popular again in the eighteenth century. Alfreds sometimes become Alf, surely one of the ugliest pet-names ever!

AMBROSE From the Greek phrase 'pertaining to the immortals': Jupiter rules the gods, and also rules the sign Sagittarius. Never very popular, it has always been used sparingly in England, and in Welsh became the pleasant *Emrys*.

CASIMIR The Polish word *kazimir* meant 'proclamation of peace' – a Sagittarian ideal. In the nineteenth century, when there were strong ties of friendship between Poland and England, it was often used; but it is now commoner in France.

CHRISTOPHER Sagittarius governs journeys, and the patron saint of travellers seems at home in this sign. Originally, the Greek term meant 'bearing Christ', and early Christians applied it to themselves. Many early British churches had murals showing the Saint, a massive man bearing the infant Christ across a ford. Now, he is the patron saint of motorists. As a christian name it became widely popular after the fifteenth century, particularly in the present century. It often becomes Chris, or Kit.

DAMIAN From the Greek 'to tame', which seems Sagittarian. Used for many centuries as a christian name in England.

DANIEL 'A Daniel come to judgement' would certainly be a Sagittarian. In England, the name has been around for over a thousand years, and has only been uncommon for the past century.

DEMPSTER In the Old English, 'a judge'. The law falls under the rulership of Sagittarius.

DOUGLAS In the original Gaelic, 'dark blue' – a Sagittarian colour. This became the name of a great and noble Scottish family, and in the sixteenth century, a christian name (at first for girls as well as boys). Spenser wrote a poem to Douglas Howard, a beautiful woman of his period.

EDGAR Though Sagittarius bears a bow and arrow, Edgar, in Old English meaning 'happy spear', has a familiar ring to the huntsman. The grandson of King Arthur was so popular a King Edgar that the name gained an impetus which carried it well down the centuries. Sir Walter Scott gave it another fillip in *The Bride of Lammermoor*.

FALKNER From the Old English: falcon hunter. No hunter could be anything but Sagittarian!

GREGORY The name, from the Greek 'to be watchful', became popular because of St Gregory, who seems to have been a very Sagittarian character – taking a great deal of the Church's money out of its coffers and using it to relieve sufferers from war, pestilence and famine, and to ransom prisoners of the Lombards. First became popular in England in the twelfth century, and has been moderately so ever since.

GUY From the Old German word for 'wide', which suggests the average Sagittarian's love of open spaces, of the broad view of things; his dislike of anything claustrophobic. Very common until Guy Fawkes, when it suddenly became unfashionable! Walter Scott's *Guy Mannering* helped to revive it for our time.

HIPPOLYTUS In the Greek, 'letting horses loose', and the horsey connection hints at Sagittarius, though the mischief might hint at Gemini. Hippolyte is common in France, but the name has not been much used in England over the past five centuries!

HUBERT Sagittarians are certainly among the most intelligent denizens of the zodiac, so a name meaning 'bright mind' belongs here! Hygebeorht, the original Old English name, died out as the ability to write became common! The name completely vanished after the fourteenth century, then as suddenly appeared again in the nineteenth century.

INIGO Christ set the child Inigo down amid the disciples, and he grew up to be a fine scholar and teacher; so he may have had Sagittarian intelligence and incisiveness. Inigo Jones, the great British architect, is the most famous bearer of the name in England, but it is still occasionally used (see J. B. Priestley's *The Good Companions*, which popularised it again in the '20s.)

IRA In Aramaic, 'the stallion'. George Gershwin's brother was perhaps the best-known modern Ira, but the name is not uncommon in the U.S.A.

JAPHET 'May he expand', in Hebrew. Sagittarians never cease expanding their minds, their estates, their ideas. The original Japhet was one of the sons of Noah, and his name was used commonly in the seventeenth century.

JASPER Sometimes as Casper, the name was said to be that of one of the three kings, or wise men (very Sagittarian); they were also astrologers, and Sagittarians sometimes have an intellectual interest in the art.

JEROME Hieronymus Sophronius, or St Jerome, must surely have been a Sagittarian, with his great learning and the love of argument which led him into so many controversies!

JUSTIN See under Libra (page 61).

KENT One derivation is 'open country', which sounds Sagittarian.

KIT A pet-name for Christopher (see page 73).

MOSES The name of the great prophet is more often used in America than England; the derivation is uncertain, so we place it here out of deference to Moses' own prophetic, wise character.

MUIR In Celtic, 'moor', which is Sagittarian country.

OSBORN 'A god-like bear', the name seems to mean in Old English; it is the bear as a hunted animal that persuades us to place the name under Sagittarius, the hunter.

PALMER A pilgrim (cf *Romeo and Juliet*, and 'holy palmers'.) Sagittarius governs all travellers.

PEREGRINE In Latin, 'traveller' or 'pilgrim' – both ruled by Sagittarius.

PHILIP 'Lover of horses', in Greek, and since one can scarcely refrain from loving (or caring for) half of oneself, the ideal Sagittarian name, Sagittarians being half horse. The apostle made the name popular, and it has always remained so (except for a short time when Philip of Spain was the great enemy of England).

RALPH A difficult name to place: it seems to come from two Old Norse words, meaning 'counsel' and 'wolf'. The first, if wise, may be Sagittarian; the second is a hunted animal, and Sagittarius is the hunter. So – The name is sometimes spelt Ralf in America; sometimes pronounced Rafe in England, rhyming with 'safe'.

ROLF 'Famous wolf' in Old German: a hunted animal? See under Ralph, above.

ROSS From the ancient *hros*, or horse. Sagittarius is half horse.

RUDOLF Stems from Rolf (see above).

SIEGFRIED From the Old German: 'victory with peace', a combination commending itself to any Sagittarian.

SIMEON 'Little hyena', in Hebrew. The hyena does not seem to be specially connected with any sign; it is certainly sometimes hunted, so we place it under the sign of the hunter.

STERLING In the Old German, 'good value; honest', good Sagittarian characteristics.

TERENCE The earliest prominent Terence was an African freed-man, the poet P. Terentius; and since there is no known meaning to the name, we place it under the sign that most values freedom.

THERRON In Greek, 'the hunter', which is definitely Sagittarian.

VALENTINE From the Latin, meaning 'strong' and 'healthy': Sagittarians have a strong natural healthiness, though they need their exercise more perhaps than the other denizens of the zodiac. The name has been used for both boys and girls.

WINSTON No known meaning for this name: so we place it here, since Sir Winston Churchill was born with the sun in Sagittarius.

ZENON A Greek name, 'from Zeus'; Zeus 'was' Jupiter, and the planet Jupiter rules Sagittarius.

YOUR SAGITTARIUS CHILD

The open, enthusiastic qualities of Sagittarian children will make them pleasant and not usually difficult members of the family. There is a powerful need for independence and freedom running through all Sagittarian veins, and it must be allowed to flow – for restriction is the main ingredient of the Sagittarian hell, and should it bring feelings of claustrophobia (psychological or physical), both young or old Sagittarians will very certainly fail to thrive, and all their lively, positive, sincere and 'uncluttered' qualities will wilt. Young Sagittarius will not like to be disciplined, and this can cause a certain amount of difficulty; but they are not lacking in good sense and logic, and will not sulk if an explanation is given of why they must conform. Then they will use their excellent intellects to cope with the situation.

Care is needed that restlessness does not become a problem. The powerful element of duality present can help young Sagittarians to cope with this. For instance, if boredom becomes apparent when they have been happily working at a favourite hobby, it is a wise parent who suggests a total change of occupation. This is the way to restore Christopher or Ingrid. A change perhaps from intellectual occupations to something more physical, and it will not be too long before they feel like getting back to the interest that made them a bit fidgety earlier.

The older they get the more they will respond to school – at first they may not like it because of the necessary routine and restrictions imposed; but as interest grows so will enjoyment. Often there is a very natural flair for languages, and this should be much encouraged. Travel is also much-loved, and if Sagittarius cannot actually be off in a 'plane, he will do so in imagination. Young Sagittarians should be encouraged to write, too: parents should make sure that a large note-pad and pencil are readily available.

'The grass is greener over the hedge' can be a Sagittarian motto, and in their enthusiasm it is possible that some inconsistency of effort can occur. This is particularly so when young, so direction is necessary. While Sagittarians are attracted to the broad overall pattern of a chosen subject in the first instance, they are not superficial; but to ensure the best development and use of potential, parents need to be on the defensive against just a few too many new and interesting projects. It is usually the challenge of a new subject that inspires achievement; 'resting on one's laurels' is not part of the Sagittarian scene.

Many girls go through a 'pony' stage, and if it is possible for the children of both sexes to learn to ride, this is particularly marvellous for Sagittarians. (Again, when young they will ride imaginary ponies if they haven't a real one!) The sporty side of Sagittarius is often over-emphasised. Many a young Centaur will enjoy his books much more than shooting arrows; indeed, it is often interesting for parents to watch the teenage Sagittarian develop, towards the end of school and in early college years, from a rather boisterous to a studious type – and when this happens the best qualities of the sign are beginning to show.

Perhaps of all the signs – if it is possible to generalise in this sensitive area – Sagittarians will be the ones to benefit most from further education, so if there is a strong desire to study in depth, all possible encouragement and assistance should be given by parents – even if they find the choice of subject a little surprising, or have apprehensions that young Christopher or Ingrid will never stick at it long enough!

Publishing, writing of all sorts, the law, lecturing and teaching at university level are among possible professions; any subjects that could lead to necessary qualifications should be encouraged.

Sagittarians are usually strong and healthy, but when young might be a little accident-prone due to their exuberance and high spirits when involved in outdoor activities. A good supply of Elastoplast dressings is recommended for those cut knees!

CAPRICORN
22nd December–19th January

GIRLS

BERNADETTE The feminine equivalent of Bernard (see below). St Bernadette of Lourdes made the name specially popular with Catholics.

BEVERLY From the Old English word meaning 'ambitious', which is a specially Capricornian attribute.

BRIDGET Probably from an ancient Celtic word meaning 'the high one', which might be a description of the average Capricorn's view of herself! St Brighid made the name popular in Ireland, and in England Bride became a common name for a while. With Mary, it is one of the two most popular names in Ireland: Bridgets often become 'Biddy'.

CASILDA A charming Spanish name which Capricorn girls might adopt, for it means 'the lone one', and they incline to be loners.

CHRISTMAS The names of Church festivals were sometimes used as fore-names, both for men and women. The sun is in Capricorn at Christmastide.

CONSTANCE From the Latin *constantia*, 'constancy': Capricornians are among the most faithful friends or lovers. One of the daughters of William the Conqueror brought the name to Britain. Often Connie, especially in the U.S.A.

ESMÉ Probably from the Latin, 'esteemed'. A name used for both boys and girls, still; originally mainly for boys, but today perhaps most often as a girl's name.

GARNET The precious stone is a Capricornian one. The name was originally used for boys, but now more commonly a girl's name.

HOLLY The association with Christmas suggests Capricorn: and the name has come to mean, traditionally, 'good luck'.

HONORIA One derivation is from the Latin *honor*, 'reputation', which all Capricorns jealously guard. Fans of P. G. Wodehouse will shudder at the name of the dread Honoria Glossop, the quintessential Capricorn, representing all that every Capricornian should determine not to become! Sometimes the name becomes Honor, which is pretty. It became, after the Norman Conquest, Nora.

IVY A Capricornian plant, which also clings faithfully to any upright support (another Capricornian trait).

KELDA From Scandinavia: 'of a fresh mountain'. Mountainous country always attracts Capricorns.

MELANIE A Capricorn colour is black, from which (in the Greek) the name springs; if ever the perennial 'little black dress' was made for anyone, it was for a Capricorn! Frenchmen brought the name over to Cornwall and Devon in the seventeenth century, and the Mayflower took it to America.

META From the Latin, 'ambitious'; Capricornian ambition is rightly legendary!

NATALIA Sometimes as Natalie, a popular name which originally meant 'Christmas Day' to the Christians who coined it from the Latin *natale*. Christmas falls in Capricorn. The name is popular in France and Russia, but is also used in England.

NONIE A pet-name for Norah (see below).

NORAH The Irish invented this pet-name for Honoria (see above).

NOREEN From Norah (see above).

PENELOPE The faithful wife of Odysseus, who waited patiently for his return from his adventures; Capricorns are usually models of faithfulness. Never extraordinarily popular as a name, but never entirely out of use.

PERPETUA From *perpetuus*, the Latin for 'continual' or 'uninterrupted'. Many people will have suffered from the latter Capricornian tendency, and many will have benefited from their constancy. A charming, now rare name.

PETRONELLA Roughly the same derivation as Peter (see page 82).

PRUDENCE From *prudentia*, in Latin, and certainly reflecting a strong Capricorn propensity. It sometimes becomes the irritating diminutive Prue. A very characteristic Capricorn name!

BOYS

AARON 'High mountain' is one derivation, and Capricorn is the sign of high places. Aaron was Moses' brother, first High Priest of Israel, and the name came to the West mainly as a Jewish forename.

ALARD 'Noble and hard', says the Old German *adalhard*; an Archbishop of Canterbury and a Saint, as well as a cousin of Charlemagne, bore the name; nowadays it is more popular in America than in Europe.

AMOS Amos comes from the Hebrew verb 'to carry'; Capricornians always have their particular burden to carry, and the minor Old Testament prophet who bore the name seemed to have his. Another name which is more popular in the U.S. than in England.

ANGUS Still a very popular Scottish name, and from the Old Irish *Aengus*, 'one choice', which certainly has Capricornian overtones.

ARTHUR While no one is certain how the name was derived, one suggestion is that it is from the Irish *art*, 'a stone', which is Capricornian enough. But perhaps it came from the Latin? Anyway, King Arthur had certain Capricorn traits: caution, method, resourcefulness, the capacity to bear hardship and to make careful plans. At first mainly popular in the West of England, around the traditional borders of Arthur's kingdom, it received a new popularity in the nineteenth century when the Duke of Wellington, the greatest modern Arthur, became famous. Tennyson's poem *In Memoriam* also helped, for it was about his dead friend Arthur Hallam; later, he wrote his long Arthurian poem, *Idylls of the King*. It is difficult to forgive H. G. Wells, who in *Kipps* popularised the awful diminutive, 'Arty'!

BERNARD Bernard, *berin hard* in Old German: 'a stern bear'! Capricorns can impress one that way! Becomes, in the feminine, Bernadette. Used in England since the Norman Conquest. Bernie, as a diminutive, seems confined to the U.S.A.

BRIAN The ancient British and Irish name for 'a hill' seems to be the origin of this name, so Capricornians will set themselves as always to reach its summit. The popular hero Brian Boroimhe made the name popular in Ireland; it reached England via Brittany in 1066, and has remained a favourite. Bretons still use it.

CECIL From Caecilius, the name of a Roman family, meaning 'blind', and suggesting a Capricorn difficulty or burden. Revived this century in England: the name of the family of the Marquis of Salisbury.

CHRISTMAS Occasionally a male forename: but see above.

CLIFFORD Originally a place-name: 'the ford near the cliff'. Capricornians love hills and high places, scrambling up them like their goat-symbols!

COMYN The Irish original, *cuimin*, or 'crooked', suggests the habitual stoop which can characterise Capricornian men.

CONAN From the Old Celtic 'high'. Several British bishops used the name in early times (it came over from Brittany at the time of the Conquest): Arthur Conan Doyle is the most famous modern Conan.

CONSTANTINE From the Latin *constans* – 'constant, firm', true Capricorn qualities. The first Christian Emperor, it is not surprising that Constantine gave his name to many babies; a Cornish St Constantine spread the name in Britain, taking it to Scotland, in particular.

DECIMUS From the Latin for 'tenth', and the most common of all the names to spring from numbers: Capricorn is of course the tenth sign of the zodiac.

DENZIL Used as a christian name by the families of William Holles and his wife Anne Denzell, from Cornwall, in the sixteenth century. The family was later very active in politics, which attracts many Capricorns.

DOUGAL The Old Irish *dubhgall* means 'black stranger', and a strong Capricorn influence in one's birth chart often gives one a very dark complexion or dark hair.

DROGO A christian name always used in the Montagu family in England, and introduced into the country at the Conquest by several of the Conqueror's followers. It comes from ancient German and Gothic, *drogo*, 'to bear or carry'; very Capricornian!

DUNSTAN The name of a remarkable Archbishop of Canterbury, Dunstan means 'hill stone' in Old English, and should appeal to Capricorns. Out of use for centuries, it came back with the Tractarians in the nineteenth century.

EBENEZER Raising a stone to commemorate the defeat of the Philistines, Samuel called it 'Ebenezer', 'stone of help'; and the accent on the final word makes the name Capricornian. Still a popular christian name in America.

ELDON 'Respected elder', in Old German.

ELI 'Height', in Hebrew – which Capricornians aspire to. A seventeenth century choice.

EMILE From a Latin root: 'striver'. The Capricornian is naturally ambitious.

EMLYN A popular Welsh name, but from the Latin, 'earnestness', suggesting a Capricornian seriousness of purpose.

ESAU 'Blind.' Not of course a Capricornian disability, particularly; but Capricorns do often have a burden of some kind to carry, and 'blindness' to some aspects of life can be a trait.

EVERARD From an Old German phrase, meaning 'a tough old boar'. Not complimentary; but Capricorns certainly have the capacity for durability!

GERARD *Ger hardu*, in Old German: 'hard spear', and the adjective suggests Capricorn. A very popular name for a century or so after the Norman conquest.

GILES The Greek original meant 'kid', and the Capricornian goat must surely once have been young! St Giles was a very popular saint in medieval times, and the name was then used for men and women. Now, men only; and not very often.

GODDARD 'A hard god', in Old German. A name which was used from the eleventh to the seventeenth century; now known only as a surname.

GUNTER A popular German name, and the origins suggest an extremely tenacious and doughty soldier. The self-preservation element of Capricorn may also have been present! Used as a christian name in England until the fifteenth century.

HECTOR The steadfast son of Priam of Troy, whose very name means 'holding fast', and who must therefore come under Capricorn. It became very popular indeed in Scotland from the thirteenth century on.

HIRAM An abbreviation of a Hebrew word meaning 'the brother is high': so the brother was more than likely a Capricorn! Hiram King of Tyre supplied cedar wood to David and Solomon, which suggests a canny businessman, too! A common name in the U.S.A., and until recently, in Yorkshire (a business connection again?).

HOWELL In Welsh, 'eminent'.

JAEL In the Hebrew, 'wild she-goat!' Originally a female name, but now used, if ever, for men.

JEREMY Originally, Jeremiah: 'may the lord raise up', as all Capricorns would like to be raised up, in their business, in their wealth, in the social scale . . . Jeremy is found from the thirteenth century, and has been much used in recent years.

JERRY Diminutive of Jeremy (see above).

LLOYD In the Welsh, *Llwyd*, or grey – a Capricorn colour.

NOEL Used as a christian name for children born on Christmas Day (which falls in Capricorn); becomes Noelle in the feminine.

OLAF Capricorns, being associated with Saturn, tend to be 'old' in character, even when they are children! Hence Olaf, from the Old Norse associated with relics and 'remains' has a Capricornian ring.

PETER Capricorn, an earth sign, also associated with mountainous rocky country, seems to suit Peter ('the rock on which I build my church.'), though he had un-Capricornian impulsiveness in his nature. One of the commonest christian names in all parts of the world.

REYNARD In the Old German, 'hard counsel', which sounds shrewdly Capricornian.

SOAMES We have found this name nowhere except in *The Forsyte Saga* of John Galsworthy, in which it was used for a man so Capricorn in nature as to convince one, almost, that the author was an astrologer!

THURSTAN An Old Danish name, which combines the name of the god Thor with the Danish for 'stone'; it is the latter element that suggests Capricorn.

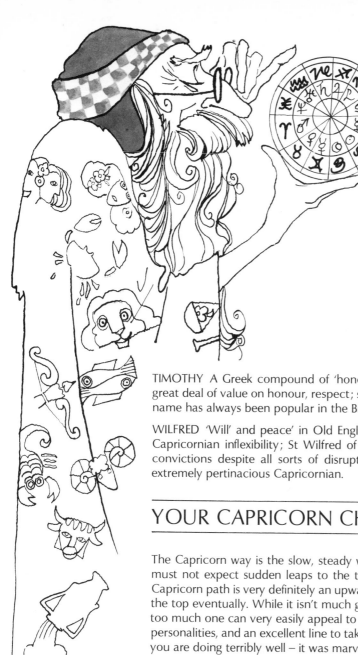

TIMOTHY A Greek compound of 'honour' and 'god'. Capricorns do place a great deal of value on honour, respect; so this seems a good placing for it. The name has always been popular in the British Isles, especially in Ireland.

WILFRED 'Will' and peace' in Old English, which suggests something of the Capricornian inflexibility; St Wilfred of Northumbria, who clung to his own convictions despite all sorts of disruptions and arguments, sounds like an extremely pertinacious Capricornian.

YOUR CAPRICORN CHILD

The Capricorn way is the slow, steady way, so parents of Capricorn children must not expect sudden leaps to the top of the school class. However, the Capricorn path is very definitely an upward one, and ambition will get them to the top eventually. While it isn't much good trying to push young Capricorns too much one can very easily appeal to the inherently ambitious area of their personalities, and an excellent line to take is the gently positive one: 'we know you are doing terribly well – it was marvellous that you beat ———— in maths, and because you *did*, we both know that you can do even better.' This line of approach should appeal. Capricorns have a marvellously off-beat sense of humour, and even the youngest can make some pretty 'old-fashioned' dry comments, especially about the family, which is important to them. Equally, they usually have some sort of burden to carry – but thrive on it; any responsibility given them will be carried out dutifully and in exactly the right way.

Parents of Capricorn children may find that they are 'loners'. They could well have one or two special friends, but are not as attracted to 'the gang' as many are. Because of this, it is sometimes the case that they are nct at their best in team games, but shine more in individual sports where they can rely on their own efforts. Athletics, high-jump, running (sometimes long-distance); also rock-climbing – these are rewarding and psychologically satisfying to them.

Capricorns are steady workers, if slowish, and will like school and its predictable routine. Generally speaking there is an inclination towards the more scientific subjects, and often ability in mathematics. Geography and geology are very often popular. Successful Capricorns often find themselves in lonely positions – as chairmen of groups of companies, perhaps – or at the least in very responsible posts where they have to take ultimate decisions. This should be remembered by parents, and letting young Capricorn take responsibility and make decisions early on is an excellent thing. It may well be that these are the best qualities of the type, and obviously they should be given every chance to develop. Initiative is not a particularly strong point in the Capricorn character, but there is plenty to counter this possible lack – determination, in particular.

The Capricorn art is music, and the children may well want a record-player at an earlier age than most. The love of music may stay at the appreciative level, but it is advisable for parents to do all they can to exploit what could prove excellent potential. In junior school Bridget and Giles may well enjoy playing the recorder, which may well be an excellent step in the right direction. If piano lessons are requested, an effort should be made to provide them – or if a more unusual instrument is preferred, this too should be encouraged, not simply because being able to play an instrument is a desirable social attribute, and perhaps a lucrative career or hobby, but because for the Capricorn it is perhaps the most perfect way to express emotion. The emotional level of a Capricorn may not be terribly high, and more than likely tends to be suppressed. Much positive release and expression can come through participating in music-making, and this is fully to be recommended.

The young Capricorn makes an excellent big brother or sister. There is usually no lack of patience, and a protective instinct will soon become apparent, and nicely expressed towards younger members of the family. But all this will be tempered with a quaint, matter-of-fact attitude, and with cool affection rather than any gushing over-emotional brotherly or sisterly love.

AQUARIUS

20th January–19th February

AQUARIUS

GIRLS

ADELAIDE From the Old German for 'noble' and 'kind': kindness, particularly, is an Aquarian habit. 'Good Queen Adelaide', William IV's queen, helped to popularise it.

AMBER Amber itself is a fossil – extremely old, therefore, like Uranus, the ruler of Aquarius!

ANN Ann, Anna, Anne, Annette, Annetta – they all spring from the cult of Anne, mother of the Blessed Virgin (though the name does not appear in the Bible). But it was Queen Anne who made the name so popular in England in the seventeenth century; so for want of a better argument, we place the name under her Sun-sign (she was born on February 6, 1665).

ANTIGONE From the Greek, 'contrary', and everyone will know at least one contrary Aquarian. The name is not too popular nowadays, though it showed some signs of revival as a result of Jean Anouilh's play about the children of Oedipus, which bore it as a title.

ASTA Perhaps best known as the name of the delicious wire-haired terrier which belonged to the Thin Man, Asta is in fact a girl's name, derived from the adjective 'venerable', which many older Aquarians become!

ASTRID A name from Norway, and from Scandinavian countries in general: in fact from an Aquarian part of the world. English families have recently adopted it, though it is in Scandinavia that it is most often found.

CELESTE From the Latin *caelestis*, 'heavenly', and Aquarius is perhaps *the* air sign, also representing space, the cosmos (what better name for an astrologer?). Popular mainly in France, but somewhat used in England.

CRYSTAL An Aquarian stone: a modern name.

DAVINA A Scottish female form of David (see page 88).

DELPHINE From the Greek, 'calmness, serenity', which are very Aquarian attributes.

EDWINA See Edwin (page 86).

ELMA Most likely a derivative of Elmer (see below).

EMMA The Old German origin suggests 'whole', 'universal', both ideals of the Aquarian Age, with its face towards world government. The first recorded Emma was a daughter of Duke Richard I of Normandy, later wife of the perhaps Piscean King Canute. Emma was much popularised by Jane Austen's enchanting heroine.

ESTELLE From the French *étoile*, 'a star', suggesting astronomy and its ruling sign, Aquarius. Dickens used the name in *Great Expectations*, but it has never been very popular.

FAITH Another of those christian names adopted from suitable nouns by the puritans after the Reformation. Faith, Hope and Charity were names often given to triplets. But faithfulness is a specially Aquarian virtue.

GERMAINE The feminine of Germanus, an extremely Aquarian saint of the seventh century, who nicely balanced theology and politics.

HANNAH The Hebrew form of Ann (see page 86); Anna was more often used until the Reformation, when Hannah appeared in England, and was popular with the Puritans (who also took it to America). A popular Quaker name; and a favourite in Ireland.

IRIS The Greek name for the rainbow, which with its airy associations, and with the visual picture of the man pouring out his pot of water in a bowed stream, seems to belong here. Fairly popular in Victorian England.

ISOLDA The original Old German name means 'Ice Queen', and this takes precedence here over the warmer less Aquarian associations with Wagner's great heroine, La Beale Isoud of the *Morte d'Arthur*. Sometimes spelt Isolde, sometimes Iseult. It was certainly Wagner who revived the popularity of the name, after many years of disuse.

JACOBA A popular Latin name for women who were really called James, and often regarded as a rather equivocal compliment; suggests Aquarian bisexuality, the whole his-and-hers idea. Nowadays, rarely enough used to be unusual.

KAY The modern association is with the Kay of Hans Anderson's *The Snow Queen*, which suggests Aquarian coolness. Sometimes used as a pet-name for Katherine (see under Libra). In Anderson, used as a girl's name; but sometimes used for boys also – Sir Kay was Arthur's Seneschal in the *Morte d'Arthur*.

MARION Mary plus Ann: Ann is Aquarian, though Mary is Virgo. Thinking of the form Marianne, and of Jane Austen's character, the name somehow seems more Aquarian than Libran, though neither fits very well. Perhaps the name should go under Gemini, since it is a double one!

NANNY From Ann (see page 86); Nancy also applies.

NINA Derived from Ann (see page 86), this version came originally from Russia, and in France became Ninette or Ninon.

OLGA Though Pisces might have a claim, since the name is from the Norse 'holy', it was originally a Russian name, so we place it here because Russia is ruled by Aquarius.

PHOEBE In Greek, 'the shining one', which suggests the rather distant film-star glamour so many Aquarians share.

ROSEANNA Rose plus Anna; see above for Ann. Rose can be either Taurean or Sagittarian; two names joined suggest Gemini – so there is a wide choice here!

ROWENA A pleasant name scarcely ever used today, this came from the Old English 'famous friend'; indeed, Aquarians do make the most constant and reliable and loving friends.

SERENA 'Calm, serene', in Latin: Aquarian properties. New England used the name considerably in the nineteenth century.

STELLA 'Star', in Latin, suggesting Aquarius because of the sign's association with astronomy, and film-star glamour.

THELMA The romantic novelist Marie Corelli invented this name for her book *Thelma: a society novel* in 1887, and it was a mark of her popularity that the name instantly caught on in England. The heroine was Norwegian, so we place it under the sign that rules Norway.

 88

THEODORA The feminine version of Theodore (see page 89).

URANIA Uranus rules Aquarius. Urania herself was the muse of astronomy.

WENDY The name was invented by J. M. Barrie for *Peter Pan*; but he said it originated with a child-friend who called herself 'Friendy', then 'Friendy-wendy', then 'Wendy'. Aquarius is the friendliest sign.

XANTHE The Greek for 'blonde': Aquarians do tend to be blond in colouring (provided the genes are right!).

BOYS

ALDOUS Probably from the Old German *aldo*, or 'old', and since Uranus (who rules Aquarius) was old enough to be Saturn's father, this seems excuse enough to place the name here. It was most popular five or six centuries ago, but is still occasionally found. The novelist Aldous Huxley was the most prominent modern example.

AYLMER The New Jersey Elmer brothers, who played such a prominent part in the American revolution, made this name popular. Its derivation, from the Old English 'noble' and 'famous' prompts its inclusion here. Tennyson helped to make it popular in England.

BONAMY From the simple French *bon ami*, or 'good friend', and an absolutely accurate description of the ideal Aquarian. Brought over from France in the eighteenth century, the name is still occasionally used in England.

BONIFACE 'Well-doer', in Latin, and much-used in the fourteenth and fifteenth centuries. Farquhar used it in his play *The Beaux' Stratagem*, for an inn-keeper; and it became in the eighteenth century a common name for publicans.

CEDRIC The novelist Sir Walter Scott seems to have invented the name for the character in *Ivanhoe*; later, Mrs Hodgson Burnett made it the christian name of Little Lord Fauntleroy, and the Victorians loved it for that reason. Scott probably meant to call his man Cerdic, after the founder of a Saxon Kingdom. That name meant 'amiable, friendly'; Fauntleroy was that, too; so are the best Aquarians.

DANA Scandinavian: and Aquarius rules Scandinavian countries.

DAVID From a Hebrew lullaby, meaning at first 'darling', but then coming to mean, simply, 'friend' (this seems to tie up with the David and Jonathan legend). Aquarius is the friendliest sign of the zodiac. Since the time of David (or Dewi), the patron saint of Wales, the name has been particularly popular there; but there were two Scottish King Davids, too. In England, used since the twelfth century. Very popular there in the 1920s and '30s, perhaps because it was the christian name of the Prince of Wales, later Edward VIII, the late Duke of Windsor. He was an Aquarian.

DURAND Aquarius guards the ancient, the old: and Durand springs from the Latin *durantem*, 'lasting'. Particularly popular with a gypsy family, the Lovells. In Italian, the diminutive is Dante.

EDWIN *Ead wine*, in Old English: 'happy friend'. The Aquarian is the friendliest denizen of the Zodiac. King Edwin was the first king of Northumberland, and the name was popular until the Conquest; then became a surname; and only recently has revived.

ELMER From Aylmer (see above).

ERNEST The meaning is the obvious one: earnestness, a prime Aquarian quality, for there is no sign to which the importance of being earnest is more marked. Late in coming into popularity, though it had been around for a hundred years before the Victorians took it up.

EZRA The name of a well-known prophet, but also from the Hebrew 'help': Aquarians are quick to do this, in any need.

FRANKLIN The Old German means 'a free man', and an Aquarian needs freedom. Coincidentally, President Roosevelt had his Sun in this sign.

GERAINT A Welsh form of the Old British, 'old'. Uranus, Saturn's father, rules Aquarius and the ancient. Geraint occurs in Tennyson's *Idylls of the King*, which slightly popularised it.

GILBERT 'Bright pledge', in the Old German; Aquarians would keep any pledge.

HARDWIN 'A hard friend', in the Old German; and while Aquarians can be good friends, they can certainly be rather hard on one at times!

HARVEY From St Harvey, an abbot and saint of the sixth century, who seems to have had a genuine Aquarian eccentricity: a blind hermit who became a monk and minstrel, and took part in various somewhat strange and no doubt legendary adventures. As Hervé, common in France.

IGOR Since Russia and Scandinavia are both Aquarian areas of the world, and since Igor is a Russian name of Scandinavian origin, what other sign could claim it? Igor Stravinsky, whatever his birth-sign, wrote extremely Aquarian music.

JACOB Amid all the argument about what this name really means, the popular idea is that it comes from the Hebrew 'he seized the heel', the heel being an Aquarian part of the body! Jacob supplanted his brother Esau, a somewhat un-Aquarian activity; perhaps he was really a Capricorn! A popular Jewish name for much of its career, but after the Restoration adopted by the Christians. Shakespeare's Iago, incidentally, was really a Jacob (and another unlikely Aquarian!).

KAY Originally a boy's name, now perhaps as often used for girls; see above.

LEOFWIN A rare name, these days, originally from the Old English 'dear friend'; and Aquarians are certainly among the friendliest denizens of the zodiac.

MUNGO In the Gaelic, 'amiable', an Aquarian epithet; popular in Scotland, particularly in Glasgow after the success of the explorer Mungo Park.

NORMAN Man of the North: Aquarius generally rules the Northern countries, Scandinavia for instance. For some time mainly Scots.

SAMUEL In the Old Norse, 'summer wanderer' or Viking, this name seems certainly Aquarian, for that sign rules the northern countries.

THEODORE Theodore of Canterbury, who made this name (which means 'God's gift') popular in England, was one of the greatest organisers and administrators of the early church, and sounds a thorough-going Aquarian.

YOUR AQUARIUS CHILD

Although it may not be a good thing for parents of Aquarian children to let them realise the fact, it is as well to bear in mind that Aquarius is the individualist of the Zodiac! There is considerable 'brightness' of one sort or another in every Aquarian and a lively attitude toward life: but interestingly they can also be quite stubborn at times. In addition to being individualists, Aquarians have rightly earned the reputation of being friendly and extremely humanitarian – they will attempt and achieve the impossible for other people. So when young Aquarians say they will do something for you, and you think they cannot possibly cope, you are very likely to be pleasantly surprised. They are marvellous at giving a helping hand, but unlike other types who are also very good at this, they are not usually motivated by emotion, but purely and simply because they recognise that the need is there, and want to do something about it. When little Emma or Ernest visits an elderly friend, it may not simply be because they feel sorry for her, but that she is ill and alone – the practical dominating over the emotional.

The generation gap between parents and Aquarian children can be more of a problem than with other types. This is because Aquarians are very often the leaders of their generation, and their ideas when young are very likely indeed to be in advance of current attitudes and opinions. So parents may experience difficulties. However, it is interesting to remember that Aquarians, once their minds are made up, may well stick to the opinions of their extreme youth until old age, not adapting as much as others; they can become very much set in their own time, rather than moving with the times.

There is an all-important need in every Aquarian for independence and free- dom. They can cope with this from an early age – which again may surprise parents. They love to develop their own life-styles, and hate them to be en- croached upon. Even within the confines of marriage or a permanent emotional relationship, they seem to have the knack of keeping an above-average amount of their own individuality – and this is right for them; but they make excellent partners, once settled, for they are extremely loyal.

At school, discipline can be ghastly for them, and they will rebel against it if they think it illogical. They may well see that it is necessary, but won't even then find it at all easy to knuckle under to it, and could well learn the hard way. An interesting streak of perversity is sometimes present: if you really *want* an Aquarian to do something for his own good – tell him to do the opposite!

There is often more than a flash of genius in Aquarians, and if this can be coaxed into a steady flame, they can do extremely well. Modern scientific subjects (astronomy, too) should be enjoyed, but in a general way there is usually an attraction to the deep past and the future. Archaeology and going on digs would be a pleasure – a study of prehistoric monsters with a view to writing a science-fiction story bringing them back to life, is the Aquarian scene! Literature and creative writing, too, are subjects to be encouraged at school.

Artistically, there is very often dramatic flair and a great love of the theatre – acting classes would be enjoyable. You may find, too, that you have a real 'modern artist' in the family, so expression through painting and drawing is excellent, if not necessarily permanent. Aquarius, being the individualist, could well be attracted to more individualist sports – champing at the bit to be old enough to learn to fly or glide, or drive a vintage car. But tolerating school sports while waiting. The choice of career is extremely varied, but there should be an element of glamour in it – be it astronaut, actress, or 'mad scientist'!

PISCES

20th February–20th March

PISCES

GIRLS

AGATHA From the Greek, 'good', which most Pisceans aspire to be! A third-century martyr with a large cult, she gave her name to many English girls born in the thirteenth and fourteenth centuries. The awful abbreviation is 'Aggie'.

ANGELA The female form of Angel. St Angela Merici founded an order of teaching nuns, which was a Piscean activity, indeed. Sometimes becomes Angelina.

ANGELICA 'Angelic', in the Latin, and first made popular in Italy by the poets Boiardo and Ariosto. The English, French and Germans took the name up in the eighteenth century (Angelica Kauffman was an English painter).

ARIADNE 'The very holy one', as the Greeks called their heroine, and the Cretans their goddess. But it was used in England just as a 'pretty name', without reference to the gods.

BENEDICTA The female form of Benedict (see page 94).

CERIDWEN The Welsh goddess of poetic inspiration: most Pisceans are poets at heart, and often on paper. Still used in Wales.

CHARITY After the Reformation, this kind of name came much into favour; and charity is a happy Piscean quality.

CHRISTIANA The female form of Christian (see page 95). Kirsty is, for once, an endearing and pretty pet-name.

CLEMENCY Sometimes Clemence, this is from the Latin *mildness*, a Piscean quality.

CLEMENTINE Feminine of Clement (see page 95). The song *Oh My Darling Clementine* did this name no good; Lady Churchill, widow of Sir Winston, is perhaps its most famous modern bearer.

CORINA One of the most popular 'poetic' names of the seventeenth and eighteenth centuries: the original Corina was a woman poet from Boeotia, and Pisces is home for the poet. Corinne is the French form, and Mme de Staël wrote a famous novel with that name as its title.

CHRISTABEL 'The beautiful christian'; though the name is an old one, it became widely popular after Coleridge's poem with the title *Christabel* at the end of the eighteenth century.

DEIRDRE 'Deirdre of the Sorrows', so, poor thing, undoubtedly Piscean! Her name occurs in the ancient *Three Sorrowful Tales of Erinn*, and many subsequent Irish poets have used it.

DOLORES Maria de Dolores, in Spain, 'Mary of the Sorrows'; the name suggests Pisces, though of course she was the Virgin Mary, and must have Virgoan connections. American Catholics often still use the name, but it is now rare in England.

EVADNE Mrs Capaneus threw herself on her husband's funeral pyre, a typically Piscean self-sacrifice. But this Greek lady's fame has not lasted until the present day, and her name is now infrequent.

EVANGELINE A popular name in the U.S.A. (Evangeline Adams was the first notable American astrologer). The noun 'evangel' suggests Pisces.

HELGA A name meaning 'holy' must be associated with the Piscean Age of Christianity. Scandinavian immigrants carried the name to America, where it is still popular, though it is less so in England.

JACQUELINE A version of the Piscean James (see page 95); sometimes, Jacquetta. Jamesina is another, perhaps rather ugly, derivative.

JEMIMA The story of Noah places Jemima, the Hebrew word for 'a dove', under Pisces: the most famous dove of all finally brought the Noah family to rest and peace. One of Charles II's love-children was christened Jemima, and it became a common name in the nineteenth century.

LOLA From Dolores (see above); mainly used in America.

NAOMI In the Hebrew, 'pleasaunce', which sounds a Piscean conception; the original Naomi was the mother-in-law of Ruth. The Puritans were fond of the name.

OPHELIA From the Greek 'to help, to succour'. In one way or another, Pisceans are in their element helping their friends, or perhaps nursing them. Shakespeare's Ophelia too has Piscean characteristics, even ending her life by drowning!

PAMELA In Richardson's novel, which gave the name great popularity in the eighteenth century, the character seems decidedly Piscean; the name seems to have been invented by Sir Philip Sidney in 1590. It is one of the relatively few 'invented' names which has remained steadily in use to the present day.

PERDITA Shakespeare invented the name for *A Winter's Tale*, apparently from the Latin root *perditus*, 'lost' (the little girl was lost, as a child). Pisceans do tend sometimes to get confused, dither, and lose themselves, mentally and sometimes geographically!

PHYLLIS 'Leafy', in the Greek; the girl who hanged herself for love (Piscean self-pity) and was turned into a tree. Used in ancient Greece and Rome, mildly popular for a while in England in the sixteenth century; in the twentieth century really popular. Phillida is a form now hardly ever seen, but charming.

PIA 'Pious' or 'devout' in Italian; occasionally found in other European countries.

TACE Sometimes written Tacye, this was a common girl's name in the sixteenth and seventeenth century, and later was popular with Quakers; it may come from 'hold your peace!' in Latin; if so, Pisceans tend to be the quietest of all zodiac people.

TALLULAH A modern American name, perhaps even invented by Miss Bankhead? One meaning, however, is 'running water', which would certainly place it firmly under Pisces.

TATIANA An early martyr, about whom little is known. All the early Tatianas seem to have been connected with the Church, and as no derivation of the name is possible, we place it under the Christian zodiac sign (the fish was a symbol of the early Christians, and can be seen drawn on the walls of the Roman catacombs; similarly, the Age of Pisces coincided with the Christian era). A favourite name in Russia, and latterly used in England (perhaps under the influence of Tolstoy, or of Tchaikowsky's heroine of *Eugene Onegin*).

TRISTA In the Latin, 'woman of sadness'. Many Pisceans seem to carry about with them their own cloud of melancholy.

URSULA The famous legend of Ursula and her eleven thousand virgin martyrs (which might seem an excessive number even for a Piscean) popularised the name as an early Christian choice, so we place it under the Christian sign (see under Tatiana, above).

VERA From the Russian word for 'faith', which makes it Piscean in nature. Two Victorian novelists (one of them the fabulously popular Ouida) used it in their best-known books, and it was much used in England in the early years of the present century.

VALERIE A name used particularly to denote Christian resignation and purity, helpfulness and friendship, so placed under the Christian sign.

VERONICA The name was given to the woman who wiped Christ's face at the time of his agony, and found the cloth impregnated with his image. So it was much used by early Christians, and is placed under the Christian sign (see under Tatiana, above).

BOYS

ABSALOM A great favourite during the twelfth and thirteenth centuries, the name of the unhappy son of David and Michal was used by Chaucer, among other writers; it has not been much used since, but derives from the Hebrew phrase for 'the divine father is *peace*' – hence, Pisces.

ADRIAN From the Latin, *Hadrianus*, meaning 'from the Adriatic Sea' – so certainly a 'watery' name; then, the name of several Popes, and the Christian age coincided with the Piscean age, so this seems a reasonable attribution. The only English Pope, Nicholas Brakespear, took the name Adrian IV, and popularised it for a while in the British Isles.

AUSTIN Sometimes Augustine, the name comes from the Latin for 'venerable' or 'consecrated'; it was very common in England in the Middle Ages, probably because of St Augustine, first Archbishop of Canterbury. Austen has now become a fairly common surname.

AUGUSTUS Like Augustine, from the Latin *augustus*, 'venerable'. Some Europeans took it up after the Renaissance, and the Hanoverians introduced it into England: it became Gus or Gussy, though these were more usually the diminutive of the girl's name Augusta.

BAPTISTE Widely used in France, from the Latin 'one who baptises' – the water association suggests Pisces. Now only occasionally used in England, but much in Canada, and in Roman Catholic countries.

BARNABAS The Hebrew 'son of consolation' suggests the Piscean, always ready to listen and help. St Paul's companion gave his name to many Englishmen after 1200, sometimes as Barnaby (in Dickens' *Barnaby Rudge,* for instance); one of the characters in the musical *Hello Dolly!* has recently helped re-establish it.

BENEDICT From the Latin *benedictus*, blessed. The Piscean age coincided with the Christian, and the suggestion is obvious. Many surnames derive from it; but it has always been used as a christian name – Shakespeare made the hero of *Much Ado About Nothing* a Benedict, though he is Geminian to a fault!

BENJAMIN 'The son of my sorrow', the youngest son of Jacob was called; Pisceans sometimes have a deep vein of sorrow in their characters. Benjamin Britten is perhaps the most famous modern holder of the name; Benjamin Franklin one of the most famous of all historical Benjamins. There has recently been a revival: the popular pet-name is Ben.

CHRISTIAN From the Latin *christianus*, 'a christian'. The sign of the fish became the sign of the secret Christians in the catacombs of Rome, where it can still be seen scrawled on walls.

CLEMENT 'Mild' or 'merciful' in the Latin: the name of a saint, and in character a Piscean one. 'Clem' is sometimes a pet-name: Clement Attlee, a Prime Minister of Britain during the 1940s, was perhaps the best-known modern Clement.

COLUM The Irish name derives from the Latin for 'dove', a peaceful symbol which suits Piscean characteristics.

CRISPIN See under Taurus.

GODFREY The Old German means 'peaceful god'; The Piscean's preoccupation is always with peace. Used in England since the Norman invasion.

HAMISH A version of James (see below), much used in Scotland.

HERON Of unknown origin, the name seems originally to have meant 'holy name', which suggests Pisces, the most religious sign.

JAKE In the Hebrew, 'pious', and an unlikely Piscean name for all those belligerent American Westerners who bore it.

JAMES James the Greater, the apostle, was not only a fisherman, but carries a cockle-shell as an emblem, which seems to make him firmly Piscean (apart from the Christian connection). Many of the pilgrims from England to the shrine at Compostella gave the name to their children, and it became enormously popular in the Middle Ages, especially in the North Country, and also in Scotland. The accession of James Stuart made it even more so.

JOB 'The persecuted.' It must be admitted that Pisceans quite often carry about with them a sense of being persecuted and worn down by (often imaginary) misfortune. Not that Job's misfortunes were anything but real! Never common as a christian name, but quite often used in the English West Country.

JOEL Of many christian names this one was particularly Christian: 'Jehovah is God', in the Hebrew; it merits inclusion under the Christian sign. Known now mainly in the U.S.A.

JOSIAH 'May Jehovah heal.' Healing, nursing, is a peculiarly Piscean career and occupation.

LEVI The father of the priestly tribe, in the Bible, and temperamentally Piscean.

SEBASTIAN Almost any martyr might seem to have Piscean tendencies; poor Sebastian, patient under his cloud of arrows, seems Piscean *par excellence*!

SOLOMON 'Man of Peace', in the Hebrew; this, and the reputation for wisdom which goes with it, seems to indicate Pisces; almost exclusively a Jewish name.

TADHGH An Irish name meaning 'poet', and Pisces is the most poetic sign.

TOBIAS 'Good', in the Hebrew – in the Christian sense, so we place it here (see under Tatiana). Tobias is sometimes now rendered as Toby, a pleasant name.

YOUR PISCES CHILD

The Piscean child is gentleness and sensitivity personified, and in upbringing will only respond to the same qualities. Scold a Piscean harshly and there will only be tears and lack of self-confidence. Usually if a Pisces child is naughty or does wrong, it is for very good, unselfish reasons, and their kindly motivation makes them difficult to correct. However, correct them one must − but very gently and very carefully. Finding a lost kitten on the way to school and trying to find its owner will make young Vera or James late: a 'good' kind of 'naughtiness'; a tendency to day-dream may also make them forgetful or careless about possessions, and discipline may be necessary there. Irresponsibility about the practical side of life may make training a young Piscean a problem at times.

These children are marvellous brothers and sisters, because of their delightful gentleness, but parents must be quite sure that they are able to cope with the practical side of taking younger members of the family for outings, for instance, before giving them the responsibility of doing so − otherwise the family will arrive home at night, having had a marvellous time, but missing the last 'bus!

The Piscean child has a very high emotional level, and this must be used and developed creatively; if it isn't, it can be wasted, or more unhappily can just contribute to escapism. We strongly advise all forms of artistic expression for Pisceans: dancing classes (often 'free movement' is enjoyed rather more than the restrictive discipline of classical ballet − though the latter is terribly good for them), painting, drawing, poetry. Quite frankly, it doesn't matter if no *real* talent is there, as long as there is a good end-product and enjoyment in the execution of the work, for in this way positive expression is achieved. If there *is* potential, even better.

It is an excellent thing for the parents of young Pisceans to plan a full out-of-school schedule for their children, so that the regular routine of, say, going to dancing (or ice-skating, which is also marvellous for them), going to help out at a nearby farm, or pet-shop, or doing jobs for some neighbour who needs help, all builds up a steady routine which in itself is a form of discipline fairly strict in structure but not the kind of 'Thou shalt not' training needed by some types.

Favourite subjects at school − other than the purely creative − are likely to be where the imagination is allowed scope. Essay- and story-writing are likely to be popular, and the enjoyment of literature will be paramount. History too could be high on the list of favourites − but in this, as in most subjects, our young Pisceans will probably be told to *concentrate*: so difficult, so *boring*! Much nicer to fantasise about that lovely king and queen all those years ago. . . . What were they really *like*? What did they actually *do*? How beautiful and romantic it must have been. . . .

It is sometimes the case that the most difficult thing for all Pisceans is to keep in touch with reality, and the best way for them to learn to do this is by, from an early age, helping people who are less fortunate than themselves. Doing work for charitable organisations helping, say, old people or children, is marvellous; and being shown exactly what good their efforts have done is equally important for them. It is all a question of trying to keep the little Piscean feet firmly on the ground, and this will not be at all easy for parents; but their problems are of a subtler nature than for many with children of other, stronger types. Finding a career for Pisceans need not be difficult: basically, any work that has some form of artistic content is excellent. Creativity can be used in the fashion world, for girls; both sexes make marvellous photographers; the medical profession and nursing are often popular. The sea, too, can attract.

Index of Boys' Names